The King's Peas

Delectable RECIPES *and Their* STORIES
from the AGE OF ENLIGHTENMENT

Published by the Gardiner Museum to accompany the exhibition
Savour: Food Culture in the Age of Enlightenment

Gardiner Museum, Toronto: October 17, 2019–January 19, 2020
Wadsworth Atheneum Museum of Art, Hartford, Connecticut: February 29, 2020–May 24, 2020

The King's Peas

Delectable RECIPES *and Their* STORIES
from the AGE OF ENLIGHTENMENT

Meredith Chilton, C.M.

With contributions from Markus Bestig,
Executive Chef, The York Club, Toronto

Gardiner Museum, Toronto
Arnoldsche Art Publishers, Stuttgart

CO-PRESENTING SPONSORS

Sincere thanks to our Co-Presenting Sponsors, whose generosity has made possible the exhibition *Savour: Food Culture in the Age of Enlightenment* and the accompanying cookbook, *The King's Peas.*

Tom Kierans & Mary Janigan
Noreen Taylor & David Staines

LENDERS TO THE EXHIBITION

We are grateful to all the lenders who have shared their works of art and enriched the exhibition *Savour: Food Culture in the Age of Enlightenment* and the accompanying cookbook, *The King's Peas.*

Institutional lenders:
Canadian Opera Company, Toronto, Ontario
Corning Museum of Glass, Corning, New York
Gardiner Museum, Toronto, Ontario
Lewis Walpole Library, Yale University, Farmington, Connecticut
    (*Wadsworth Atheneum Museum of Art venue only*)
The Metropolitan Museum of Art, New York City, New York
The Museum of Fine Arts, Boston, Massachusetts
New York Academy of Medicine Library, New York City, New York
    (*Wadsworth Atheneum Museum of Art venue only*)
Royal Ontario Museum, Toronto, Ontario
Sterling and Francine Clark Art Institute, Williamstown, Massachusetts
Thomas Fisher Rare Book Library, University of Toronto, Ontario
    (*Gardiner Museum venue only*)
University of Toronto Art Centre, Toronto, Ontario
Wadsworth Atheneum Museum of Art, Hartford, Connecticut
Winnipeg Art Gallery, Winnipeg, Manitoba
Yale Center for British Art, New Haven, Connecticut

Individual lenders:
Chris Antemann
Michele Beiny
Ivan Day
Dr. William Johnston
Janet Panabaker
Rosalie Wise Sharp
Alan Shimmerman
Madame Tricot (Dominique Kaehler Schweizer)
Private collectors who wish to remain anonymous

Contents

OPPOSITE: Two woodcock tureens, Germany, Höchst, c. 1750. Tin-glazed earthenware (faïence). Metropolitan Museum of Art, New York. The Lesley and Emma Sheafer Collection, bequest of Emma A. Sheafer, 1973

Preface

In *The Art of Cookery Made Plain and Easy* of 1747, author Hannah Glasse advised her readers on the preparation of green vegetables. She writes: "Most people spoil garden things by over-boiling them. All things that are green should have a crispness, for if they are over-boiled they neither have any sweetness or beauty." This call for freshness, authentic flavours, and mouthwatering presentations in one of the most popular cookbooks of the eighteenth century echoes the sensibilities of today's foodies. *The King's Peas* and the exhibition it accompanies, *Savour: Food Culture in the Age of Enlightenment*, unveil these long-forgotten and surprising connections between then and now. They present the period as a transformative moment in the history of food and dining in France and England, a time when many of our current concerns, discourses, and practices find their roots—from ethical food choices to the cultivation of produce in challenging climates.

The King's Peas is a perfect albeit unexpected companion for *Savour*, an exhibition that celebrates the symbiosis between the objects and the delicious food they contained while capturing the humour and personalities of the period. An innovative take on the traditional catalogue, this cookbook–social history hybrid presents recipes gleaned from seventeenth- and eighteenth-century publications, interpreted for modern use by the author and richly illustrated with objects featured in the exhibition, from ceramics and silver to rare cookbooks and contemporary knitted art. We thank Markus Bestig, Executive Chef at The York Club, Toronto, for contributing four recipes to this book.

Savour features outstanding works of art, and we are grateful to all the institutions and private lenders for sharing their treasures with our public, as well as to the participating artists: Chris Antemann, Ivan Day, Loraine Krell, Janet Panabaker, and Madame Tricot (Dominique Kaehler Schweizer). Exhibition designer Gerard Gauci contributed a unique theatrical vision to the exhibition with his whimsical and majestic *trompe l'oeil* paintings. We also acknowledge the participation of the Wadsworth Atheneum Museum of Art, Hartford, where this exhibition will be presented following its debut at the Gardiner Museum, Toronto.

Above all, most sincere thanks to the exhibition curator and author of this book, Meredith Chilton, C.M., Curator Emerita at the Gardiner Museum, for sharing decades of research on the history of dining in a deeply informed yet playful and accessible narrative.

Grey partridge tureen and stand, Germany, Hannoversch-Münden, c. 1770. Tin-glazed earthenware (faïence). Courtesy of Michele Beiny

Her masterful storytelling is sure to captivate the food lovers of our day and inspire the adventurous cooks among them.

Finally, this project would not have been possible without the generosity of our Co-Presenting Sponsors: Tom Kierans and Mary Janigan, and Noreen Taylor and David Staines. We thank them for their unwavering support as we celebrate the profound love of food that shapes our lives and who we are.

Karine Tsoumis, PhD
Curator, Gardiner Museum

Food Culture
in the AGE OF ENLIGHTENMENT

Meredith Chilton

Food and dining were transformed in Europe during the Age of Enlightenment, and this transformation continues to resonate today. What many of us eat now, how it is cooked, and how we dine continues to be influenced by radical changes that occurred in France from the 1650s until the French Revolution in 1789. Of course, further changes occurred in subsequent years, but this small cookbook focuses on the time when French cooking and dining began to sweep triumphantly through Europe (fig. 1).

Over thirty recipes from French and English cookbooks of the period appear in *The King's Peas* to give a taste of the past. Each one is accompanied by stories and snippets of history along with curious objects for your enjoyment. The whole is intended as a delectable feast for the eyes.

FIG. 1 Folding fan (painted in the manner of François Boucher), Austria or Germany, 1760s. Leaf: gouache and bronze painting on paper, mother-of-pearl decorated with gold-and-silver toned metal leaf. Pivot: green paste jewel. The Metropolitan Museum of Art, New York City. Robert Lehman Collection, 1975. Full image on p. 16

The fascination with food that so grips us now also predominated in the 1700s. Nicolas de Bonnefons describes it perfectly. He was a French gardener and valet to King Louis XIV and the author of two important books: the first on gardening, followed by one on cooking called *Les délices de la campagne* (The delights of the countryside). He declares, "Of all the senses, there is nothing more delicious, nor more necessary to life than that of taste"[1] (fig. 2). The ephemeral pleasures of food had become such a passion that even princes and members of the nobility tried their hands as amateur cooks. For instance, Louis XV had a small kitchen in his newly created *petits appartements* (the king's private apartments) at Versailles and rustled up an omelette for his close friends on occasion. His cousin, the Louis-Auguste II de Bourbon, Prince de Dombes (1700–1755), is attributed as the author of a curious small cookbook. This may not sound unusual to us now, but at the time it was unprecedented for the nobility to perform such tasks. These noblemen and their fellow epicures were the foodies of their times.

Although Italian cooking had a profound impact on that of France in the 1500s, French cooks took the lead from 1650 onwards. Key chefs, including François Pierre de La Varenne, Vincent La Chapelle,

Menon, and François Marin, established the French style of cooking (fig. 4). Through the publication and translation of their cookbooks, French cooking came to dominate taste across Europe. Even in Italy, French cuisine reigned supreme in the 1700s. When Giacomo Casanova was entertained to "a choice and delicious dinner" by his mistress in Venice in 1753, he exclaimed that "the cook must be French, and she said I was right."[2] However, it was not until the 1800s that French cooks such as Marie-Antoine Carême and Auguste Escoffier gained the "celebrity chef" recognition that some chefs enjoy today.

It is curious that male cooks dominated in France, while in England a number of important cookbooks were written by women for ladies, housekeepers, cooks, and servants (fig. 3). Chief among them was Hannah Glasse (1708–1770), whose cookbook *The Art of Cookery Made Plain and Easy* was first published anonymously in 1747 and went through at least thirty editions over the next hundred years. Hannah Glasse had little time for French chefs or expensive French cooking, which she described as "the blind folly of this age." She believed that with the help of her cookbook, "every servant who can but read will be capable of making a tolerable good cook"[3] (fig. 5). Despite her efforts, expensive French cooks replaced many

FIG. 3   *The good housewife*, Germany, Meissen, c. 1755–1760. Model by Johann Joachim Kändler (1706–1775). Hard-paste porcelain, enamels, and gilding. The Alan Shimmerman Collection

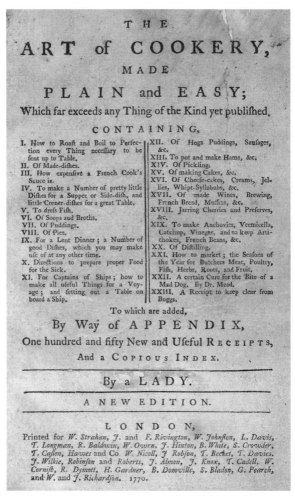

English ones in wealthy households as the century progressed, and the fashion for French cuisine spread.

Changes to food culture began in the kitchen garden. At Versailles, Louis XIV acquired the services of Jean-Baptiste de La Quintinie (1626–1688), a gifted horticulturalist who transformed the palace's kitchen gardens between 1678 and 1683 (fig. 6). De La Quintinie was able to expand the growing season of many vegetables and fruits using Italian techniques of enclosures, raised warm beds, and glass cloches to protect tender young plants, as well as the careful selection of seeds. His work resulted in the expansion

of available fruits and vegetables for the royal kitchens; for instance, forty-seven different types of pears were cultivated at Versailles, enabling the serving of fresh pears almost year-round (fig. 7). Gardeners all over Europe copied these methods.

Diets of the wealthy in the 1600s and 1700s were not limited to the produce of farms and gardens. Long-established European trade in wine, olive oil, cheese, preserved meat and fish, and even pasta supplemented local foodstuffs. Exploration and colonialism expanded the horizons of trade to Asia and the New World, leading to increasing imports of new foods, such as turkeys, tea, chocolate, spices, and especially sugar. The quest for lucrative locations to grow sugar further fuelled colonization. For example, to gain back the valuable island of Guadeloupe and its sugar cane, France ceded almost all of its vast Canadian territories to Britain under the terms of the Treaty of Paris of 1763. The all-consuming addiction to sugar had devastating human consequences, with the enslavement and

FIG. 7   Follower of Luis Meléndez (1716–1780),
Still Life with Fruit, c. 1750. Oil on canvas.
Collection of the Winnipeg Art Gallery

FIG. 8 John Atkinson (active 1770–1775), *Kitchen Scene*, 1771. Oil on canvas. Yale Center for British Art, New Haven, Connecticut. The Paul Mellon Collection

transportation of millions of Africans to toil on sugar and chocolate plantations in the Americas.

Products obtained from trade were found alongside locally grown foods in the markets and kitchens of Europe. In the kitchen, technological advances enabled more sophisticated culinary techniques. Key was the widespread adoption, in the houses of the wealthy, of brick stoves with rows of hobs fuelled by charcoal. These stoves enabled the temperature control necessary for sauces, which were central to French cuisine (fig. 8). Mechanized spits replaced manual

operation. Cooks gave great attention to detail, providing instructions for cooking and presenting their food. Even Hannah Glasse advised, "Always be very careful that your greens be nicely picked and washed ... Most people spoil garden things by over-boiling them. All things that are green should have a little crispness, for if they are over-boiled they neither have any sweetness or beauty."[4]

New philosophies for healthy eating were proposed in Europe during the Age of Enlightenment. It is remarkable to find that *nouvelle cuisine*, made famous in the 1970s by French chefs such

as Paul Bocuse and Michel Guérard who advocated freshness, flavour, and healthy choices, had already appeared in the late 1730s! English scientist John Evelyn (1620–1706) proposed a vegetarian "herby diet" in 1699, and, in the 1760s, Jean-Jacques Rousseau expounded it as his philosophy (fig. 9). Rousseau advocated a simple, meatless diet based on fresh, local foods, believing that being closer to nature was healthier for body and character.

Along with the refinement of cooking came dramatic developments in the arts of the table. Meals were served in three or more courses *à la française* (in the French style) during this time. Depending on the event and the complexity of the meal, servants or members of the household arranged all the serving dishes in a symmetrical pattern on the table, course by course (fig. 11). Even simple meals were presented in this manner. We now wonder how people of the

FIG. 11   Martha Bradley (dates unknown), A Table for a Wedding Supper, *The British Housewife: or, the Cook, Housekeeper's and Gardiner's Companion*, vol. 2. London: S. Crowder and H. Woodgate, 1760. Collection of Ivan Day

OPPOSITE: FIG. 10   Étienne Jeaurat (1699–1789), *The Poet Alexis Piron at the Table with His Friends Jean-Joseph Vadé and Charles Collé* (detail). Oil on canvas. Musée du Louvre, Paris, France

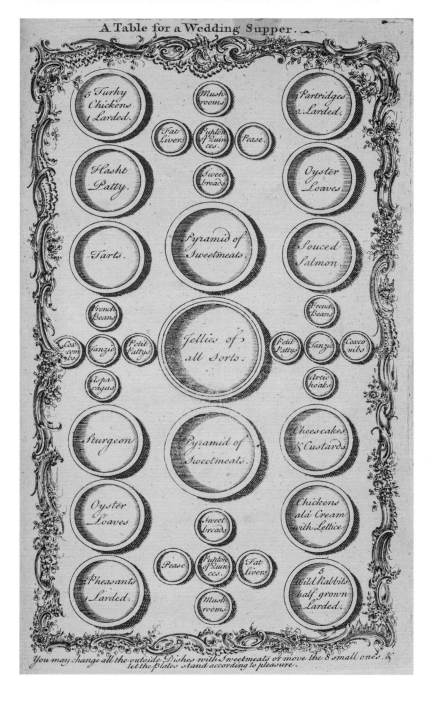

period ate so much at grand dinners, but at the time, diners chose food only from the selection of serving dishes placed closest to them on the table. If they wished to eat something placed out of easy reach, a servant would fetch it. Dining in the French manner became the height of style all over Europe, and both the bourgeoisie and the upper classes adopted it with enthusiasm.

Whether diners ate from dishes of gold, silver, or pewter depended on their rank and financial status. Gold was restricted to kings and their immediate families; silver could be used by princes, the nobility, and members of the bourgeoisie whose wealth was sufficient; while pewter or tin was used by everyone else (fig. 12). Faïence and porcelain were first used only for the dessert course because their surfaces were impervious to acidic fruit juices, but as the 1700s progressed, entire dinner and dessert services were made of porcelain—the new material of the age. Porcelain was a material that transcended rank and could be used by anyone with means. Even people of modest income owned ceramics, and sometimes porcelain (fig. 10).

The combination of new foods and the formal presentation *à la française* led to the development of purpose-specific dishes for

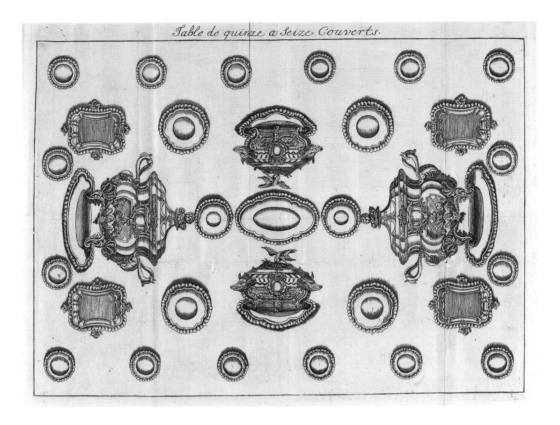

FIG. 13   Vincent La Chapelle (d. 1745), Table of Fifteen to Sixteen Covers, *The Modern Cook: Containing Instructions for Preparing and Ordering Publick Entertainments for the Tables of Princes, Ambassadors, Noblemen, and Magistrates*, 3rd ed., vol. 3. London: Printed for Thomas Osborne, 1736. Collection of Ivan Day

OPPOSITE: FIG. 12   Étienne-Jacques Marcq (c. 1705–1781), Tureen and cover, France, Paris, 1749. Silver. The Metropolitan Museum of Art, New York City. Robert Lehman Collection, 1975

Table de quinze a Seize Couverts.

serving and eating. In the 1700s, there was a veritable landslide of new vessels for both savoury and sweet dishes that made eating more elegant and more complicated. In 1742, chef Vincent La Chapelle suggested it was necessary to have twelve different-sized and -shaped dishes along with a range of elaborate tureens to serve his food—a sharp contrast to François Massialot, who, thirty years earlier, recommended just four different sizes of simple circular dishes (fig. 13). This new development probably related to the impact of advances in cooking as well as the rise of consumerism. Silver and ceramic manu-

factures created new vessels for the most fashionable foods, such as cups for ice cream and sauceboats for savoury or sweet sauces.

For a short time in the mid-1700s, there was a craze for naturalism. All kinds of forms, from teapots to tureens, were made to look like animals, birds, or vegetables. It is tempting to imagine how steam might emerge from the nostrils of a faïence boar's head tureen when it was filled with hot ragout, but it is unlikely that such complex pieces were actually used to serve food (fig. 14). Sometimes ceramic eggs or vegetables appeared on the table, perhaps to fool or entertain guests.

FIG. 15   Jean-François de Troy (1679–1752), *The Oyster Luncheon* (*Le déjeuner d'huîtres*), 1735, Oil on canvas. Musée Condé, Chantilly, France

OPPOSITE: FIG. 14   Boar's head tureen, France, Strasbourg, Paul Hannong, c. 1748–1754. Tin-glazed earthenware (faïence). Private collection

Times for eating varied from country to country, and from city to countryside. The hours for fashionable dining by the wealthy became flexible during the 1700s in France. In the first part of the century, a light breakfast (*déjeuner*), usually consisting of a bowl of broth or a hot drink with a little bread, was eaten at about nine or ten o'clock. Dinner (*dîner*), the principal meal of the day, was served in the afternoon at around two o'clock. Supper (*souper*) or a light collation was taken late in the evening. As the century progressed, dinner gradually became a later event. It was often served by candlelight, and a new meal—luncheon (confusingly called *déjeuner* in France)—gradually became a midday feature (figs. 15 and 16). Because of this, *souper* was largely abandoned in favour of *dîner*, *déjeuner* became lunch, and breakfast was renamed *petit déjeuner*, reflecting its small size. Interestingly in French Canada, which was lost by France to England in 1763, the earlier French terminology for meals is still in use by Canadian francophones: *déjeuner*, *dîner*, and *souper*.

Just as dining habits have changed in recent times with the adoption of much more casual eating, so it was in the 1700s. The great theatrical formality of the French court under Louis XIV in

FIG. 16   Michel Barthélémy Ollivier (or Olivier) (1712–1784), *Dinner of the Prince de Conti (1717–1776) in the Temple*, 1776. Oil on canvas. Château de Versailles, France

the 1600s led to a reactionary desire for informality and intimacy during the reign of his successor, Louis XV, in the following century. Dinners became more sophisticated and informal, and intimate meals emerged as part of the new quest for privacy (fig. 17). Sometimes servants were dispensed with completely in the dining room, and diners served themselves to both food and wine.

Towards the end of the 1700s, the first restaurants began to appear in Paris. Before then, upper-class travellers with letters of introduction could be invited to dine at the houses of local aristocrats, but others were obliged to eat at inns, where the *table d'hôte* (the host's table) was offered at a communal table with little or no choice of food. The *table d'hôte*, sometimes now called the *prix fixe*, is

FIG. 17 Isidore Stanislas Helman (1743–1806/1809) after Jean-Michel Moreau the Younger (1741–1814), *The Gourmet Supper (Le souper fin)*, 1781. Engraving. Musée de la Ville de Paris, Musée Carnavalet, Paris, France

still found in restaurants today. Street vendors and cheap eating houses also provided cooked food to the working classes in large cities, offering local specialities from macaroni in Naples to meat pies in London.

Food culture underwent radical changes during the Age of Enlightenment. Gardeners adopted new methods of horticulture, enabling a wider selection of vegetables and fruits to be grown for longer seasons. French cooks introduced lighter, more refined, and healthy cooking in the middle of the century, and their cuisine gained supremacy in Europe. Even the arts of the table transformed, along with social changes that brought in a quest for privacy and new hours for dining. In many ways, the 1650s to 1790s were a precursor to modern times.

Many of us have experienced a radical change in the availability of ingredients, with refrigeration and efficient transportation bringing foods from faraway parts of the globe. It is now possible to enjoy a breadth of international and ethnic cuisines largely unknown in the Western world fifty years ago. The philosophies of food have changed, often in favour of healthier and more moral choices. Even the way we eat has undergone radical transformation

as many of us, once again, favour less formal dining experiences. We have become obsessed with food and dining—modern foodies who reflect the passion for gastronomy that consumed gourmets in the Age of Enlightenment.

Delectable RECIPES AND Their STORIES

Soups

Pumpkin or Butternut Squash Soup

Menon was one of the most influential French cookbook authors of the mid-1700s. Nothing is known of him—even his full name—apart from his extensive published works. He was a proponent of the revolutionary *nouvelle cuisine* that advocated simplicity, flavour, and good health through the selection of quality ingredients, careful technique, and uncomplicated presentation. This recipe is taken from his most popular cookbook, *La cuisinière bourgeoise*, intended for middle-class female cooks.

Potage à la Citrouille (Pumpkin Soup)

Menon (dates unknown), *La cuisiniere bourgeoise*, 1756, vol. 1, pages 27–28

"According to the size of the soup you wish to make, take a large or small pumpkin or squash; for a pint of milk you need a quarter of a medium pumpkin; remove the skin and the seeds, cut the pumpkin into small pieces and put it in a large saucepan with water, and cook for two hours until it is reduced to a marmalade and almost no water remains. Add a piece of butter the size of an egg and a little salt and cook for a few more minutes. Bring a pint of milk to the boil and add some sugar, judge the amount yourself; pour the milk into the pumpkin. Take your serving dish and arrange some sliced bread inside; moisten with some of the pumpkin soup, then cover the dish and place it on some hot cinders until the bread has become soaked, but don't let it boil. Then add the rest of the hot soup."

OPPOSITE: Pehr Hilleström (1732–1816), *En piga höser såppa uter en kiettel* (A Maid Taking Soup from a Pot), late eighteenth century. Oil on canvas. Location unknown

Butternut Squash Soup

Inspired by Menon's recipe
6 servings

This soup has a subtle and delicious flavour and is very simple to make.

INGREDIENTS

1½ lb (680 g) peeled butternut squash, weighed after it is peeled and seeded
1 generous oz (30 g) butter (the original recipe says it should be the "size of an egg")
1 heaped tsp (6 g) kosher salt
Black pepper to taste
2 cups (500 ml) 3.25 % (full fat) milk
1 tbsp (15 g) sugar

METHOD

· Cut the peeled squash into approximately 1 in (2.5 cm) cubes. Place in a large saucepan and just cover with cold water. Bring to a boil. Simmer gently for about 15 to 20 minutes until the water is mostly absorbed and the squash is soft. Add the butter and let the mixture simmer for another minute or two while stirring. Add salt and freshly ground black pepper to taste.
· Heat the milk and sugar in a separate saucepan until it is steaming but not boiling.

- Purée the squash mixture with an immersion blender, or in a blender or food processor. Then carefully stir the heated milk into the squash mixture. Adjust the seasoning to taste.
- To reheat, return the soup to a saucepan over a gentle heat. Do not let the mixture boil.
- Serve the soup with fresh bread and butter or dried bread croutons.
- The original recipe, as with many French recipes of the time, calls for the soup to be served with a large slice of bread, over which the soup is poured. Croutons are suggested as an alternative. Do not season the bread or croutons—the flavour of the soup is very subtle.

Croutons

INGREDIENTS
2 thick slices stale white bread, crusts removed, or
2 soft bread rolls, crusts do not need to be removed
  if they are soft; cut into cubes
2 tbsp (30 ml) sunflower oil, or equivalent light oil

METHOD
- Preheat oven to 325 °F (165 °C).
- Place the cubes on a baking sheet and, using your hands, toss with oil. The goal is to give the bread a little oil here and there, not to saturate it with oil. Bake for 10 to 15 minutes until the bread is dry and a light golden brown. Check the bread often—do not burn! Toss the cubes about halfway through cooking so they are browned on more than one side.

Soup and *Pumpkins*

Soup was eaten by everyone in Europe, from kings to peasants. The wealthy would indulge in a wide variety of different soups at both dinner and supper; even Louis XIV was reported to have eaten no fewer than "four full platefuls of different kinds of soups" at one sitting.[5] The most extravagant soup of them all was called olio, consisting of a remarkable number of different meats, fowls, game, and vegetables.

François Pierre de La Varenne (1618–1678), the father of modern French cooking, listed no fewer than fifty-eight different soups in his highly influential cookbook of 1651, *Le cuisinier françois*, including two for pumpkin.[6] La Varenne's recipes were frequently copied by later chefs, such as Menon, whose version of pumpkin soup is almost identical to that of La Varenne.

Hester Bateman (1708–1794), Ladle, England, London, 1790–1791. Silver. Collection of Dr. William Johnston

OPPOSITE: Kate Malone (b. 1959), *Pumpkin*, 2002. Crystalline-glazed stoneware. Courtesy of Michele Beiny

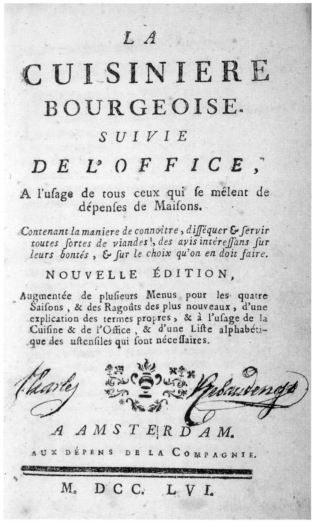

Menon (dates unknown), Title page, *La cuisiniere bourgeoise*, new ed. Amsterdam: aux dépens de la Compagnie, 1756. Thomas Fisher Rare Book Library, University of Toronto

Garbure, a Vegetable Soup from Gascony

Vegetable soups of cabbages, root vegetables, and dried pulses were the main diet of the poor, along with bread. It is unusual to find such a soup among the recipes of the Prince de Dombes's cookbook, *Le cuisinier gascon* (The Gascon cook), but it was considered a traditional dish of the region. He enriched it with a rich meat stock, bacon, chicken, and goose legs, ingredients that were out of the reach of many. Any available or seasonal vegetable may be added to this dish.

Potage de Garbure (*Garbure* Soup)

Louis–Auguste II de Bourbon, Prince de Dombes (attributed), *Le cuisinier gascon*, 1747, pages 181–182

"Cook some beef, veal, lamb, and a mixture of ham, once cooked moisten with good bouillon & place in a large marmite: then put in all kinds of vegetables, such as cabbage, parsnip, carrots, turnips, celery, leeks, onions, parsley root, a bunch of sorrel, a handful of dried peas, a good bouquet garni, three cloves of garlic, plenty of seasoning, a little bacon, some sausage. You put in two marinated and blanched goose thighs, one chicken, and once everything tastes good, take some rye bread that you simmer so it tastes good, arrange the goose thighs and the sausage and bacon on top, and serve the vegetables blanched, the bouillon underneath."

OPPOSITE: Goose tureen, France, Strasbourg, c.1750. Tin-glazed earthenware (faïence). The Metropolitan Museum of Art, New York City. The Lesley and Emma Sheafer Collection. Bequest of Emma A. Sheafer, 1973

Garbure Soup

Inspired by the Prince de Dombes's recipe
8 servings

INGREDIENTS
Other vegetables, such as turnips, parsnips, spinach, etc., may be added.
1 tbsp (15 ml) oil
1 tbsp (15 g) butter
2 large yellow onions, sliced
1 leek, carefully cleaned and sliced
2 stalks of celery, sliced
3 cloves garlic, sliced
1/2 cup (125 ml) wine
6 cups (1,400 ml) chicken stock
1 tsp (5 ml) apple cider vinegar
8 oz (227 g) slab smoked ham, cut into cubes
8 medium carrots, peeled and sliced
2 cups (250 g) butternut or other squash, peeled and cubed
1 1/2 cups (355 ml) canned beans (such as cannellini, navy, etc.), drained and rinsed
10 baby potatoes
Large stalk thyme, with many sprigs
2 bay leaves
1 tbsp (2 g) mixed Herbs de Provence, or mixed herbs
2 cups (200 g) shredded green cabbage
Freshly ground pepper
2 confit duck legs, optional
Fresh country or rye bread

METHOD

- In a large casserole, melt the butter and oil over a medium heat. Add the onions, leek, and celery, cooking well until they just begin to brown. Add in the garlic and cook for another minute. Deglaze with the wine and add the chicken stock and the apple cider vinegar.
- Add in the ham, carrots, squash, rinsed beans, potatoes, thyme, bay leaves, and herbs. Bring to a boil and then simmer for 40 to 60 minutes. Add the shredded cabbage and cook for 5 minutes or longer, depending on your taste. Remove bay leaves and thyme. Season to taste with freshly ground pepper. Serve with the bread.
- Optional: Heat the duck legs in a separate saucepan over a medium-high heat for 10 to 12 minutes until hot and the fat is rendered. Remove the legs from the pan (reserve the duck fat for another use) and gently separate the flesh from the bones, discarding the bones and the skin.
- To serve, place some cooked duck meat in each bowl and spoon the soup over the top.

Revolutionary Potatoes

Spanish conquistadors brought the first potatoes to Europe from Peru in the late 1500s. Potatoes were slowly adopted by many European countries for feeding animals, and very gradually for human consumption. Many people remained suspicious of the tuber—a popular rumour in France said that if you ate potatoes, you would catch leprosy. By the 1750s, potatoes were eaten in England, Germany, Ireland, and elsewhere in Northern Europe, but it was not until the French Revolution that potatoes were widely accepted in France. This was largely thanks to the tireless efforts of Antoine-Augustin Parmentier (1737–1813), who had encountered potatoes while incarcerated in a German prisoner-of-war camp. Parmentier realized that potatoes could be a viable solution to frequent famines in France caused by the failure of wheat and rye crops, even if potatoes could not be made into bread.[7]

Nicolas-Bernard Lépicié (1735–1784), *Preparing a Meal*, before 1784. Oil on canvas. Musée des Beaux-Arts, Rennes, France

OPPOSITE: Madame Tricot (Dominique Kaehler Schweizer, b. 1948), Various vegetables, 2019. Hand-knitted wool. Collection of the artist

Chilled Asparagus and Pea Soup

There were specific times and days during the year when Catholic adherents refrained from eating meat, as well as rich, sweet or fried foods. Fasting days included Lent (the forty days before Easter) and all Fridays. Many French cookbook writers divided their recipes between those suitable for fasting and those for non-fasting days. Menon specifies this recipe for Asparagus and Pea Soup as suitable for fasting.

Potage d'Asperges à la purée verte en maigre (Asparagus Soup with Green Purée, for fasting)

Menon (dates unknown), *La cuisiniere bourgeoise*, 1756, vol. 1, pages 35–36

"First make a bouillon of roots [see below]; once it is sieved, take some to cook a cup of green peas; take some asparagus of medium size, which you will use to garnish the soup, cut them into three-finger lengths; blanch them quickly in boiling water, and remove them into cold water; tie the stalks into small bunches, and cut off the tops; cook the stalks with the peas, and once the peas are cooked, make them into a purée; mix the soup with the root bouillon and make a garniture on the side of the dish with the asparagus tips; when serving add a coulis of peas."

Bouillon de racines (Bouillon of Roots)

Menon (dates unknown), *La cuisiniere bourgeoise*, 1756, vol. 1, page 34

"Put a piece of butter in a casserole with three sliced onions, two root vegetables, a parsnip, a piece of celery, three leeks, all cut into small pieces; half a clove of garlic and two cloves. Cook them all until they are a little coloured, then add water and boil for an hour, pass your bouillon through a sieve and season with salt."

Chilled Asparagus and Pea Soup

Inspired by Menon's recipe
4 generous servings

INGREDIENTS

Vegetable stock:
6 cups (1,400 ml) water
4 stalks celery
3 large carrots
1 large leek, well rinsed to remove any internal dirt
1 large onion, cut into quarters, studded with two cloves
1 clove garlic
1 bay leaf
Large sprig thyme
6 or more parsley stalks
6 peppercorns

Soup:
1 lb (450 g) fresh asparagus
2 cups (280 g) frozen or fresh young peas (defrost if frozen)
1 tbsp (3 g) fresh mint leaves, minced finely
Kosher salt and freshly ground black pepper, to taste
1/2 cup (125 ml) 15% (single) cream

Olio tureen and stand (*pot à oille Saxe* or *ordinaire*), France, Vincennes, c. 1754–1755. Model attributed to Jean-Claude Duplessis (1699–1774). Painted by François Binet (1730–1775). Soft-paste porcelain, enamels, and gilding. Royal Ontario Museum, Toronto. Purchased with funds provided by the Steven George Leggett and Suzanne Leggett Fund and the Frank and Emily Riddell Memorial Fund

METHOD

- To prepare the vegetable stock: rinse and then chop celery, carrots, and leek into uniform pieces. Place chopped vegetables in a large saucepan with water and boil with the onion, bay leaf, garlic, thyme, parsley, and peppercorns. Skim, then simmer for 1 hour, or until the vegetables are soft. Strain and discard the solids. There should be 4 cups of stock. (Alternately, use 4 cups [950 ml] of high-quality, unsalted commercial vegetable stock.)
- Snap the bottom of the asparagus stalks and discard the woody ends; rinse. Boil 3 cups (700 ml) of the vegetable stock in a saucepan with a generous pinch of salt. Add the asparagus and boil until just tender-crisp, no more than 2 minutes. Immediately remove the asparagus with a slotted spoon, and plunge into a basin of cold water. Reserve the stock.
- Cut about 1½ in (4 cm) off the tips of the asparagus spears and reserve as a garnish for the finished soup.
- Return the stock to a boil; cut the remaining asparagus stalks into inch-long pieces. Add them to the stock and simmer until they are fork tender. Add the defrosted or fresh peas, bring back to a boil, and simmer for a minute until all the vegetables are soft. With an immersion blender, purée the vegetables and stock to make a very smooth soup. Add additional stock to thin the soup to taste. Season with salt and freshly ground black pepper. When soup is cold, stir in the cream and the minced mint.
- Serve chilled, garnished with the blanched asparagus tips.

Vincent La Chapelle (d. 1745), Fold-out image opposite title page, showing a large olio tureen, *The Modern Cook: Containing Instructions for Preparing and Ordering Publick Entertainments for the Tables of Princes, Ambassadors, Noblemen, and Magistrates*, vol. 1. London: Printed for Thomas Osborne, 1736, 3rd ed. Collection of Ivan Day

Soup Tureens

Before the invention of tureens, soup came to the table in two bowls, one containing the soup and the other inverted over it. A napkin was tied around both to hold them together. This unsatisfactory method of transportation ended with the invention of the earliest soup tureens made of silver in the early 1690s. These were followed by examples in porcelain, once the method of production was discovered in France, Germany, Austria, Italy, and England.

Tureens were the grandest dishes on the dinner table. They always appeared at the first course to serve soup. A special circular form of tureen was used to distinguish olio, the richest and most complex soup of all. Tureens of differing sizes were also used for subsequent courses to serve "made" dishes, such as fricassees and ragouts. Services consisting only of tureens in silver and porcelain were made before whole dinner services appeared in porcelain.

Provençal *Cabbage and Cheese* Soup

The other great French chef of the mid-1700s was François Marin, who, along with Menon, introduced a new style of cooking which they called *cuisine moderne* and *nouvelle cuisine*, respectively. Just as chefs in the 1960s and 1970s, Marin and Menon rejected their predecessors' overly elaborate cookery in favour of refined and lighter dishes with an emphasis on subtle flavours and nutritious ingredients. Here, Marin proposes a recipe reminiscent of a French onion soup, topped with a thick slice of bread and melted Gruyère cheese.

Potage aux choux & au fromage à la Provençale
(Provençal Cabbage and Cheese Soup)

François Marin (dates unknown), *Suite des dons de Comus*, vol. 1, 1742, pages 110–111

"Blanche the cabbage; cook it in water & then boil with some butter, a little salt and oil. When the cabbage is cooked, simmer with your bouillon; cut a large loaf of bread into slices, make a bed of bread and place on top a bed of mild Gruyère cheese; then put cracked pepper on your bread and wet it with very good oil. Once well simmered, serve garnished with your cabbage, and a little attached to the dish."

Provençal Cabbage and Cheese Soup

Inspired by Marin's recipe
6 servings

INGREDIENTS
1 small Savoy cabbage
1 tbsp (15 ml) oil
2 tbsp (30 g) butter
2 medium yellow onions, thinly sliced
2 large cloves garlic, chopped
3 tbsp (30 g) flour
1 cup (250 ml) white wine
6 cups (1,400 ml) chicken stock, or bouillon
1 large stalk fresh thyme with many sprigs
1 bay leaf
1 small onion, peeled and studded with 3 cloves
Kosher salt and freshly ground black pepper, to taste
6 thick slices crusty white or wholewheat bread
1 lb (450 g) Gruyère cheese, grated

METHOD

- Shred a small cabbage into strips, removing and discarding the core and any thick stems. Rinse cabbage well, then in a saucepan of boiling salted water blanch it for 1½ minutes (no longer). Remove the cabbage immediately, plunge into a large bowl of ice-cold water, and let drain in a colander.

- Melt butter and oil in a large, deep saucepan or casserole over a medium heat. Add the sliced onion and cook until soft and beginning to brown. Add the garlic; stir and cook for 1 minute. Now shake in the flour, stir until it is well combined, and cook for 2 minutes. Gradually add the wine, stirring constantly. Then add the chicken stock and bring to a boil. Add the herbs and the small whole onion with the cloves. Simmer for 20 minutes, letting the liquid reduce a little. Add the cabbage, return to a boil, and simmer for another 15 to 20 minutes until the cabbage is tender. Remove the whole onion and the bay leaf. Season to taste with salt and pepper.

- Cut 6 thick slices of crusty white bread and toast under the broiler. Dish the soup into heat-resistant bowls. Place a slice of bread on top of each filled bowl and cover with cheese. Season with ground black pepper. Broil for a few minutes until the cheese is hot, bubbly, and slightly browned.

Gardener with a watering can, Switzerland, Zurich, c. 1770. Hard-paste porcelain, enamels. Gardiner Museum, Toronto. The Hans Syz Collection

OPPOSITE: Cabbage tureen, France, Strasbourg, Paul Hannong, c. 1744–1754. Model attributed to Johann Wilhelm Lanz (active 1748–1761). Tin-glazed earthenware (faïence). Private collection

The Problems of *Little Gnawing Animals*

Nicolas de Bonnefons, a noted gardener and cookbook author of the mid-1600s, tells us there were so many different types of cabbage that it would be difficult to have them all in one garden. His personal favourites were the "large-sided" cabbages, which were ready to eat in the fall: "To my Gusto there is no sort of Cabbage comparable to them, for they are speedily boyled and are so delicate, that the very grossest part of them melts in one's mouth."[8] However, it was not only humans who found cabbages delicious: "There are several little Animals which gnaw, and indamage Cabbages ... as a certain green hopping Flie, Snails, Ants, the great Flea, etc. The best expedient I finde to destroy these *Insects* is, the frequent watering."[9]

It is possible that the splendid cabbage tureen illustrated on page 43 was used as a table ornament. To function, it would have needed an inner liner to protect its complex form from hot soup or ragout. Tureens with naturalistic forms were at the height of fashion in the mid-1700s.

Pair of snail tureens, France, Strasbourg, Paul Hannong, c. 1750–1754. Model by Johann Wilhelm Lanz (active 1748–1761). Tin-glazed earthenware (faïence). Courtesy of Michele Beiny

Eggs
AND
Cheese

Swiss-Style Stuffed Omelettes

This recipe for rolled omelettes filled with spinach and Parmesan comes from *Le cuisinier gascon* (The Gascon cook), a cookbook attributed to Louis-Auguste II de Bourbon, Prince de Dombes (1700–1755), the grandson of Louis XIV and his mistress Françoise-Athénaïs de Montespan. The prince describes himself in the tongue-in-cheek, extravagantly worded introductory epistle as "one of the best Cooks of France."[11] Omelettes were extremely fashionable during the 1700s. They appear in most cookbooks, spelled in a wide variety of ways—here, in *Le cuisinier gascon*, they are called "omeletes." Most entertaining is the "Hamlet" that appears in Mary Smith's cookbook *The Complete House-keeper, and Professed Cook* of 1772.

Omeletes farcies à la Suisse (Swiss-Style Stuffed Omelettes)

Louis-Auguste II de Bourbon, Prince de Dombes (attributed), *Le cuisinier gascon*, 1747, pages 34–35

"Make half a dozen 'omeletes' with six eggs & a little cream, seasoned, a little salt; make them thin and large; once made, make an ordinary stuffing of sorrel, finished, you add to it some grated Parmesan, a few white bread crumbs, several minced hard-boiled egg yolks, and mix them all together. Place your omelettes on a napkin & stuff and roll them; once rolled, take a dish of the size you wish ... arrange your omelettes cut into two in the base of the dish, and put more stuffing in the spaces between them, with a little cream; you have an omelette without stuffing that you put on the top as a cover, grate it with Parmesan and sprinkle with a little melted butter, & place in the oven for half an hour: once cooked with a good colour, serve hot."

The prince recommends the dish be served with thin slices of baguette, soaked in a little egg and fried, that can be placed around the stuffed omelettes.

Stuffed Omelettes in the Swiss Style

Inspired by the Prince de Dombes's recipe
3 servings for lunch or supper

INGREDIENTS

Filling:
12 oz (350 g) fresh baby spinach, or sorrel, rinsed
1 tsp (5 g) unsalted butter
½ cup (50 g) freshly grated Parmesan cheese
4 tbsp (12 g) fresh bread crumbs
2 hard-boiled egg yolks, minced
¼ cup (60 ml) 15 % (single) cream
Kosher salt and freshly ground black pepper, to taste
Pinch of freshly grated nutmeg, optional

Omelettes:
A little unsalted butter, for cooking
6 large fresh eggs
¾ cup (175 ml) 15 % (single) cream
Kosher salt and freshly ground black pepper, to taste

To finish:
Generous ½ cup (50 g) freshly grated Parmesan cheese
Toasted baguette

Hen and chicks tureen, France, Sceaux, c. 1755. Tin-glazed earthenware (faïence). The Metropolitan Museum of Art, New York City. Gift of R. Thornton Wilson, in memory of Florence Ellsworth Wilson, 1954

METHOD

- To prepare the filling: rinse the spinach and place the drenched leaves in a saucepan with no other water. Bring to a boil and cook for a few minutes until all the spinach has wilted. Remove to a colander and press with a wooden spoon or a potato masher to remove excess water. Chop the spinach.
- Melt the butter in a saucepan and add the cooked, chopped spinach, the Parmesan, bread crumbs, egg yolks, and cream. Season well with salt and freshly ground pepper. Add a little freshly grated nutmeg if desired. Cover and keep warm.
- To prepare the omelettes: in a small bowl, whisk together 1 of the eggs, 2 tsp (10 ml) of the cream, salt, and freshly ground pepper to taste. Melt a very small knob of butter in an omelette pan with an inner flat surface of approximately 8 in (20 cm). Pour the egg mixture into the pan, swirling to cover the entire bottom surface of the pan. After cooking for 1 or 2 minutes, loosen the edges of the omelette and carefully turn over; cook for another minute and then turn the omelette out onto several sheets of paper towel. Repeat for each omelette and stack the cooked omelettes, one on top of the other, until all 6 omelettes are made.

Chicken and egg seller, Germany, Meissen, 1753–1754. Model attributed to Peter Reinicke (1715–1768). Hard-paste porcelain, enamels, and gilding. The Alan Shimmerman Collection

- To finish the dish: butter an ovenproof dish, 9 × 9 in (23 × 23 cm). Preheat the oven to 325 °F (165 °C). Divide the filling into half. Fill the first omelette with approximately 2 tbsp (30 ml) of the filling, placing the filling in a line close to one edge, and then roll up the omelette. Place the rolled omelette in the middle of the dish. Repeat with the next 5 omelettes, placing the filled, rolled omelettes side by side in the dish.
- Now with the remaining filling, make a border of spinach around the edges of the pan, leaving the rolled omelettes in the middle. Cover with freshly grated cheese.
- Bake for 15 minutes, then broil until the top is bubbling and golden brown.
- Serve with toasted baguette and a fresh green salad.

'Burnt to a Crisp

The Prince de Dombes was not the only noble amateur cook of the time. In 1726, a small "laboratory" containing a patisserie oven and several individual stoves was installed in Louis XV's private apartments at Versailles. Occasionally, he prepared his own omelettes, something utterly unheard of during the reign of his predecessor, Louis XIV.[12] In her memoirs, Madame du Barry wrote that the king once cooked and served an omelette for a small group of intimate friends: "The guests looked at each other with an air of consternation; nevertheless Louis XV proceeded to help each person to it, and then, taking a part himself, he said, 'It is rather burnt, to be sure, but still quite eatable.'"[13]

After Maurice Quentin de La Tour (1704–1788), *Louis XV (1710–1774), King of France and Navarre*, after 1730. Pastel on paper. Musée Antoine Lecuyer, Saint-Quentin, France

Ramequins, or Cheese Puffs

Menon gives valuable information about cheeses in *La cuisinière bourgeoise*. He begins by talking about well-ripened cheeses made with both goat's and cow's milk, then mentions Brie, which was easily found in Paris, and cheeses from Brittany, Languedoc, and Holland. Menon says that Gruyère must be chosen with large holes, and then mentions Parmesan, and Roquefort, which is "esteemed above all, and by consequence is the most expensive." He includes little cream cheeses eaten with sugar and cream, which are still enjoyed in France today. But of all cheeses, he says only Parmesan, Gruyère, and Brie are used in cooking. Menon then goes on to give a recipe for *ramequins*—little cheese choux pastry puffs made with Brie.

Ramequins

Menon (dates unknown), *La cuisiniere bourgeoise*, 1756, vol. 2, page 150

"For this put a good piece of Brie and crush it in a casserole with a piece of butter about the size of a *quarteron*, a *demi-septier* of hot or cold water, very little salt and a chopped anchovy. Boil this all together & put in enough flour to drink it up, dry this on the fire until your dough is quite thick, put it into a different saucepan and add enough eggs for the dough to absorb without becoming liquid, the dough must not gain any colour.

Make little pieces of dough the size of a pigeon's egg and put them on a sheet, and cook them in the oven. To be well done the *ramequins* must be light and of a good colour."

OPPOSITE: Madame Tricot (Dominique Kaehler Schweizer, b. 1948), *A basket of cheeses*, 2019. Hand-knitted wool. Collection of the artist

Cheese Puffs

Inspired by Menon's recipe
Yields about 40 as an appetizer

INGREDIENTS
⅝ cup (150 g) all-purpose flour
1 tsp (5 g) salt
½ tsp (2 g) cayenne pepper
½ cup (125 ml) water
3 oz (85 g) Brie, cut into small pieces
3 oz (85 g) butter
1 anchovy, chopped
4 large eggs, whisked just before adding
¾ cup (75 g) finely grated fresh Parmesan cheese

METHOD
· Preheat oven to 375 °F (190 °C).
· Sift flour with the salt and cayenne pepper, place on a piece of parchment paper, and set aside. In a saucepan with the water put the Brie, butter, and anchovy; stir and melt all together. When the Brie has melted, sieve the mixture, pressing down on the solids. Return to the saucepan and bring to a boil. Remove from

heat and immediately add all the flour mixture in one quick movement. Beat the mixture vigorously with a wooden spoon until it is smooth and forms a mass in the middle of the pan. Cool until it is warm, but not hot.

· Now whisk the eggs and add little by little to the dough, beating each time very vigorously with a wooden spoon so the egg is well incorporated. The resulting dough should be shiny, smooth, and thick enough to hold its shape.

· Place the parchment paper, or silicone baking sheet, on a baking sheet (you will cook two sheets' worth of puffs, one sheet at a time). With two small spoons, make individual balls about 1 inch

(2.5 cm) in diameter, place at least 1½ in (4 cm) apart. Finish by generously covering puffs with grated Parmesan.

· Bake for 15 to 20 minutes until puffed, golden brown, and crisp on the exterior. Remove cooked puffs from the baking sheet and let cool on a rack. Pierce each puff with a skewer to help steam escape.

· While the first sheet is baking, repeat preparation of puffs for the second sheet.

· Best served on the same day, within a few hours of baking, while they are still crisp. They can also be stored in a lidded container for up to four days and crisped in the oven for a few minutes at 300 °F (150 °C) before eating.

New Philosophies for Food

Not only was cooking transformed in the mid-1700s but so too were philosophies about food. The *cuisine moderne* and *cuisine nouvelle* introduced by François Marin and Menon mirrored new thoughts about healthy eating, simplicity, and returning to nature. Jean-Jacques Rousseau advocated a startlingly modern meatless diet of local, seasonal foods, including vegetables, fruit, cheese, eggs, fish, and bread prepared in the simplest possible ways. He advised that seasoning should be kept to a minimum and sauces abandoned. "If I am given milk, eggs, salad, cheese, brown bread, and ordinary wine I am sufficiently entertained." He believed that staying close to nature meant that both human morals and the spirit remained uncorrupted by society.[10]

The Cow (*La vache*), France, Sèvres, c. 1759–1760.
Model by Étienne Maurice Falconet (1716–1791) after
Jean-Baptiste Huet (1745–1811). Soft-paste biscuit
porcelain. Private collection

Vegetables,
Salad,
AND *Pickles*

The King's Peas

Nicolas de Bonnefons, a French gardener and valet to King Louis XIV, was the author of two important books: the first on gardening, followed by one on cooking called *Les délices de la campagne* (The delights of the countryside). In the introductory epistle to the first volume, he declares, "Of all the senses, there is nothing more delicious, nor more necessary to life than that of taste."[16] He goes on to give very emphatic advice about flavour: "A cabbage soup should taste like cabbage, a leek soup like leeks, a turnip soup like turnips; the same applies to all other vegetables."[17] This was a change from earlier tastes, which favoured strong spices and complex mixtures of ingredients.

Des pois de toutes sorts (Peas of All Kinds)

Nicolas de Bonnefons, *Les delices de la campagne, suite du jardinier françois…*, 1684, pages 146–147

"The younger the more excellent they are … This [recipe] is for shelled peas. They can be fricasseed as well: brown the butter, lard or fat in a saucepan, then throw them in with a little water to cook them, season them with Salt and Spices and some Parsley and Chives chopped together; if you like, add two sprigs of Thyme and Marjoram, to ensure they add only to the taste, tie them with a string and remove them completely before serving. To make the sauce, sweet Cream is marvelous, but it must not be added until the end of the cooking."

Sweet Young Peas

Inspired by Nicolas de Bonnefons's recipe
4 servings

As fresh peas out of season are almost as rare now as they were in the in the 1660s, this recipe calls for frozen peas. However, tender, young fresh peas can be substituted if available.

INGREDIENTS
2 sprigs each of fresh thyme and marjoram (if not available, use a smaller amount of fresh oregano), tied together with a piece of string
Pinch of sugar
1 cup (250 ml) water
2 cups (280 g) frozen peas
½ cup (125 ml) of heavy or whipping cream, warmed
1 tbsp (3 g) thyme and marjoram leaves, chopped together
1 tsp (1 g) chopped fresh parsley
1 tsp (1 g) snipped fresh chives
Kosher salt and freshly ground black pepper, to taste
1 to 2 tsp (3 to 6 g) instant blend flour, optional

Pea pod, England, Derby, c. 1770. Soft-paste porcelain, enamels. Gardiner Museum, Toronto. Gift of Mr. and Mrs. J. H. Moore

METHOD

· Add the tied bundle of herbs and a pinch of sugar to the water in a small saucepan. Bring to a boil and add the frozen or fresh peas. Return to a boil, reduce heat, and cook for 1 or 2 minutes, or until the peas are cooked to taste. Drain the peas in a colander and remove the herb bundle. Add the warmed cream and the chopped thyme and marjoram. Stir and season to taste with salt and freshly ground pepper. Reheat very gently.

· If a thicker sauce is desired, shake in a little instant blend flour and reheat gently. Serve on a warm dish. Sprinkle with the snipped parsley and chives.

Children shelling peas, England, Chelsea, c. 1759–1770. Soft-paste porcelain, enamels, and gilding. Museum of Fine Arts, Boston, Massachusetts. Gift of Richard C. Paine

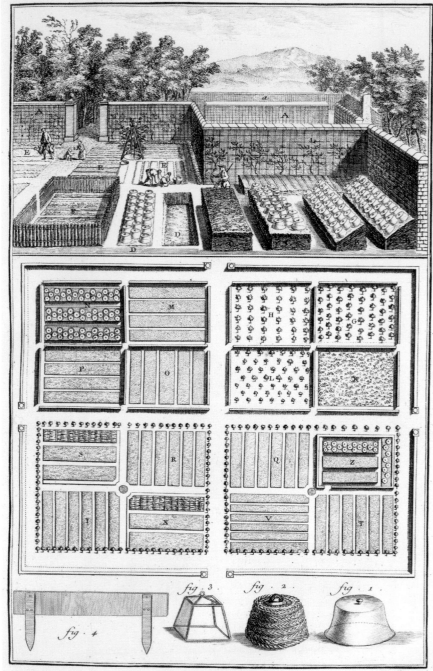

Agriculture,
Jardin Potager, Couches.

The King's Peas

We are so used to eating a wide variety of vegetables year-round that we forget how their availability depends on the seasons. On January 16, 1660, a French spy returning from a mission to Italy caused a sensation at Versailles. He presented King Louis XIV with a small basket of fresh peas. The king's entourage exclaimed that "nothing like them, in that season, had ever been seen in France!"[18] The Comte de Soissons quickly shelled the peas and the king's principal cook, Sieur Baudoin, was summoned to cook the rare treat for the king's delectation. Fresh young peas remained popular at Versailles: Madame de Sévigné noted, "There is no end to this interest in peas ... Some ladies sup with the king, and sup well at that, only to return home to eat peas before retiring, without any care for their digestion."[19]

Perhaps it was these out-of-season peas that inspired King Louis to employ Jean-Baptiste de La Quintinie (1626–1688), the brilliant gardener who created the kitchen gardens at Versailles in 1678. De La Quintinie adopted Italian methods of forcing fruits and vegetables, enabling the king's favourite vegetables and fruit to be grown for extended seasons. Eventually, the vegetable gardens at Versailles influenced others all over Europe.

Denis Diderot (1713–1784), Agriculture, Kitchen Garden, Beds, *Encyclopédie, ou Dictionnaire raisonné des sciences, des arts et des métiers.* France: André le Breton et al., 1751–1766. Engraving on paper, c. 1770. Private collection

Fire-Roasted *Asparagus*

Shocked by the lack of interest among the English in eating vegetables, the Italian scholar and humanist Giacomo Castelvetro (1546–1614) wrote a treatise on Italian horticulture while living in London in 1614. In it, he describes all the vegetables, herbs, and fruits of Italy by season, in the order in which they appear. In spring, he writes first about hops, followed by spinach and asparagus.

Asparagus

Giacomo Castelvetro, *The Fruit, Herbs and Vegetables of Italy: An Offering to Lucy, Countess of Bedford*, trans. Gillian Riley, 1989, page 53

"Next, or more or less at the same time [in Spring], asparagus begins to appear … Some people eat it raw, with salt, pepper and Parmesan cheese, but I prefer it cooked and served like hops, with oil, a little vinegar, and salt and pepper. Others take the plumpest spears of asparagus and having oiled them well, roll them on a plate in salt and pepper to season them thoroughly, and then roast them on a grid. Lavishly sprinkled with bitter orange juice, this makes a most delicate dish. Quite apart from being good to eat, asparagus is a most health-giving vegetable … [it] is positively helpful to those who find urinating painful."

Asparagus tureen and stand, Germany, Schretzheim, c. 1752–1800. Tin-glazed earthenware (faïence). Wadsworth Atheneum Museum of Art, Hartford, Connecticut. A. Everett Austin Jr. Collection. Gift of Mrs. Helen G. Austin, David E. Austin, and Sarah G. Austin

Fire-Roasted Asparagus

Inspired by Giacomo Castelvetro's recipe
4 servings for a first course

INGREDIENTS
1 kg (approximately 2 lb) fresh asparagus, with stalks of a medium size
Olive oil
1 large, bitter Seville orange, or 1 sweet orange and ½ small lemon
Kosher salt and freshly ground black pepper, to taste

METHOD

- Snap off the end of each stalk of asparagus; neaten the stalks by cutting them all at a similar length. Soak the asparagus for half an hour in cold water. Meanwhile, light the barbecue and bring to a medium temperature (approximately 400 °F [200 °C]). Dry the asparagus then lay it on a platter, so the stalks are all facing in the same direction, then brush all over with olive oil. Season generously with salt and freshly ground pepper.
- Carefully place the asparagus on the grill with tongs, or place the stalks in a mesh grilling basket to set on the grill. After 2 to 3 minutes, when the asparagus has grill marks, turn it and continue cooking for another 1 to 2 minutes. Taste the asparagus to test for doneness; it should be tender but still a little crisp, according to taste. The timing depends on the size of the asparagus and the heat of the barbecue.
- Juice the Seville orange, or if a bitter orange is not available, mix the juices of one sweet orange and 1/2 small lemon. Dish the asparagus onto a warm platter and pour a little of the citrus juice over the top. Serve additional juice separately.

John Atkinson (active 1770–1775), *Girl Bundling Asparagus*, 1771. Oil on canvas. Yale Center for British Art, New Haven, Connecticut. The Paul Mellon Collection

Grass or Asparagus

Asparagus was a highly esteemed vegetable in the 1600s and 1700s. Nicolas de Bonnefons in *Le jardinier françois* gave careful instructions for its cultivation, which included digging beds 4 feet square and 2 feet deep and filling them with well-dug and fertilized soil. He advised establishing three separate rows of plants and refraining from harvesting the asparagus for three or four years.[14]

John Evelyn (1620–1706), the great British horticulturist, noted that the delicate flavour of asparagus was enhanced by avoiding overcooking: "being so speedily boil'd, as not to lose the verdure and agreeable tenderness; which is done by letting the water boil before you put them in."[15] Curiously, asparagus was frequently called "sparrowgrass" or simply "grass" in English cookbooks of the period.

Nicolas de Bonnefons (dates unknown), Labourers preparing beds in a walled kitchen garden, *Le jardinier françois, qui enseigne a cultiuer les Arbres, & Herbes Potageres; Auec la maniere de conseruer les Fruicts, & faire toutes sortes de Confitures, Conserues, & Massepans,* 8th ed. Paris: A. Cellier, 1666. Thomas Fisher Rare Book Library, University of Toronto

Fried Artichokes

Artichokes were one of the most fashionable vegetables in the 1600s and 1700s. They were not only enjoyed on their own but also used frequently in ragouts and pies, and as a garnish. Nicolas de Bonnefons writes with enthusiasm about them in *The French Gardiner*, "The artichoke is one of the most excellent fruits in the kitchen garden, recommended not only because of its great bounty, and the many ways in which it can be used, but also because it has a long fruiting season."[20]

Artichaux frits (Fried Artichokes)

Louis Liger (1658–1717), *Le ménage des champs et de la ville, ou, nouveau cuisinier françois*, 1764, page 242

"To fry artichokes, cut them into slices, remove the choke and wash them well. Then you cook them in water. Once cooked, you can marinate them a little and then coat in a light batter, composed of flour, salt, pepper and an egg. Then they can be fried in a little lard or butter. You can, if you like, simply flour the artichokes once they have been dipped in a beaten egg, & then fry them. Serve them with fried parsley as a garnish."

Deep-Fried Baby Artichokes

Inspired by Louis Liger's recipe
6 servings for a snack

INGREDIENTS
2 eggs
1 tbsp (15 ml) oil
¼ tsp (1 g) salt
Ground pepper, to taste
⅔ cup (160 ml) beer (lager) or milk
1 cup (150 g) flour
2 egg whites
2 11 oz (340 ml) jars or cans brined or marinated artichokes
Safflower or similar oil for deep frying
Fresh lemon, for serving

Small artichoke tureen, France, poss. Strasbourg, c. 1750. Tin-glazed earthenware (faïence). Private collection

OPPOSITE: Madame Tricot (Dominique Kaehler Schweizer, b. 1948), *Artichokes*, 2019. Hand-knitted wool. Collection of the artist

METHOD

· Combine and whisk together the two whole eggs, oil, salt, and the beer. Sift the flour in a separate bowl, make a well in the centre, and add about ⅔ of the egg and beer mixture. Whisk the flour into the eggs, starting from the inner edges and working towards the outside. Add the rest of the egg mixture and whisk well to combine all the flour. Continue to whisk until a smooth batter is formed. Refrigerate for 2 to 3 hours. Before using, whisk the egg whites until they have formed soft peaks but are not dry and fold them gently into the batter. Rinse the marinated or brined artichokes in cold water and drain them on several thicknesses of paper towel. Pat them dry.

· Put the oil in the deep fryer, or a deep saucepan, and heat, testing until a little batter dropped into the oil immediately crisps (about 350 °F [175 °C]). Place all the artichokes in the bowl with the batter and stir so they are covered. Spoon them out, one by one, and drop into the hot oil in batches. Do not overcrowd. Turn so they are browned on both sides. When golden brown and crispy, remove onto a dish with paper towel to dry.

· Serve with lemon wedges. A tangy dip made with capers in a lemon-flavoured mayonnaise would be a good accompaniment.

After Abraham Bosse (1602/1604–1676), *The Five Senses: Taste.*
Oil on canvas. Musée des Beaux-Arts, Tours, France

Oil or Butter?

Perhaps the most famous incident with artichokes involved Michelangelo Caravaggio (1571–1610), somewhat earlier than the Age of Enlightenment. On April 24, 1604, when he was eating lunch with two friends in a Roman tavern, the hot-tempered artist ordered a plate of eight artichokes, half of them to be cooked in oil and half in butter. When they arrived, it looked as if they had all been cooked in butter. Caravaggio asked the waiter to show him which ones had been cooked in oil, and the waiter cheekily suggested that he should simply use his nose to tell the difference. This response was too much for Caravaggio, who threw the whole plate of artichokes at the waiter, cutting his face. The artist then stood and grabbed his friend's sword. Not waiting another minute, the waiter fled to the police to make a formal complaint, which is still preserved in Rome's State Archives.[21]

A Delectable Salad

John Evelyn (1620–1706), a British scientist, author, Fellow of the Royal Society, conservationist, and vegetarian, published a persuasive argument in favour of a "herby diet." In his book *Acetaria: A Discourse of Sallets*, he shows "how possible it is by so many Instances and Examples, to live on wholesome vegetables, both long and happily."[22] He identifies eighty-two plants and gives detailed instructions on how to make salad. He also includes a seasonal chart showing plants and edible flowers month by month and how to mix them together to make a delicious salad.

How to prepare Sallet

John Evelyn, *Acetaria: A Discourse of Sallets*, 1699, pages 173–174

"In the Composure of a *Sallet*, every Plant should come in to bear its part, without being over-power'd by some Herb of a stronger Taste ... but fall into their places, like the *Notes* in *Music*, in which there should be nothing harsh or grating; And tho' admitting some *Discords* (to distinguish and illustrate the rest) ... and melt them in to an agreeable Composition."

"Let your Herby Ingredients be exquisitely cull'd, and cleans'd of all worm-eaten, slimy, canker'd, dry, spotted, or any ways vitiated Leaves. And then that they be rather discreetly sprinkl'd, than over-much sob'd with Spring-Water, especially *Lettuce* ... After washing, let them remain a while in the *Cullender*, to drain the superfluous moisture; And lastly, swing them altogether gently in a clean coarse Napkin."

Mixed Green Salad

Inspired by John Evelyn's instructions
Recipe by Markus Bestig, Executive Chef, The York Club, Toronto
6 servings

INGREDIENTS
1 head Boston lettuce, washed and picked into bite-size pieces,
   approximately 3 cups (165 g)
1 cup (25 g) picked flat-leaf parsley
1 cup (90 g) thinly shaved fennel bulb, core removed
1 cup (25 g) baby arugula
1 cup (25 g) baby kale
1 cup (25 g) baby spinach
1 cup (50 g) Belgium endive, cut into bite-size pieces
1 cup (25 g) blonde baby frisée
1 cup (25 g) nasturtium flowers
1 cup (25 g) assorted mixed green hearts
$^{1}/_{2}$ cup (12 g) picked tarragon
$^{1}/_{2}$ cup (12 g) chives, cut into 1 in (2.5 cm) batons
$^{1}/_{2}$ cup (12 g) radish sprouts
$^{1}/_{2}$ cup (12 g) picked mint
$^{1}/_{2}$ cup (12 g) pea tendrils
$^{1}/_{2}$ cup (12 g) basil seedlings
$^{1}/_{2}$ cup (12 g) edible flowers

METHOD

· Prepare all the salad components by gently rinsing those that require it in a bowl of cold water, drying lightly, and placing them in a clean linen towel to rest and crisp in the fridge for half an hour. Then gently toss all the ingredients together, reserving the edible flowers, in a large bowl; make sure you have plenty of room.

· When it comes time to serve, whisk the vinaigrette to ensure it is emulsified and add little by little to just dress the salad. *

* See pages 66–69 for Executive Chef Markus's vinaigrette recipe.

Cos lettuce tureen and stand, England, Longton Hall, c. 1755. Soft-paste porcelain, enamels. Courtesy of Michele Beiny

The *Herby* Diet

John Evelyn tried to convince his readers of the benefits of his "herby diet," though he admits it was an uphill struggle. Along with reasons of health, temperance, and frugality, he adds the moral argument to spare cruelty to animals, citing both God and ancient philosophers, and writes a hymn to Nature:

"Nature, who has given to *Plants* such astonishing Properties; such fiery Heat in some to warm and cherish, such Coolness in others to temper and refresh, such pinguid *Juice* to nourish and feed the Body, such quickening *Acids* to compel the Appetite, and grateful *Vehicles* to court the Obedience of the Palate, such *Vigour* to renew our natural Strength, such ravishing *Flavour* and *Perfumes* to recreate and delight us ... What shall we add more? Our Gardens present us with them all."[23]

Pietro Longhi (1701–1785), *In the Gardens at the River Mouth*. Oil on canvas. Ca' Rezzonico, Museo del Settecento, Venice

Godfrey Kneller (1646–1723), *Portrait of John Evelyn (1620–1706)*, c. 1687. Oil on canvas. The Royal Society, London

Oxoſeon, or Vinaigrette

It is the marriage of salad ingredients with the vinaigrette that makes a salad sing. Once again, John Evelyn gives careful instructions for his *intinctus* or *oxoleon*, the names he gives to his vinaigrette. He notes that vinegar is the sweetest of all condiments, perhaps because it "incites Appetite, and causes Hunger, which is the best Sauce."[24] A number of different peppercorns were available in Europe and America during the 1600s and 1700s; Evelyn calls for "a Pod of Guiney-Pepper" in this recipe. This is also known as long pepper, which is now little used. It has a more subtle, complex, and spicier taste than black pepper, though both look the same when crushed.

Oxoleon

John Evelyn, *Acetaria: A Discourse of Sallets*, 1699, pages 121 and 177

"Your *Herbs* being handsomely parcell'd, and spread on a clean Napkin before you, are to be mingl'd together in one of the Earthen glaz'd Dishes: Then, for the *Oxoleon*; Take of clear, and perfectly good *Oyl-Olive*, three Parts; of sharpest *Vinegar* (*sweetest of all Condiments*) *Limon*, or Juice of *Orange*, one Part; and therein let steep some Slices of *Horse-Radish*, with a little *Salt*: Some, in a separate *Vinegar*, gently bruise a *Pod of Guinny-Pepper*; ... then add as much *Tewksbury*, or other dry *Mustard* grated, as will lie upon an Half-Crown Piece: Beat, and mingle all these very well together; but pour not on the *Oyl* and *Vinegar*, 'till immediately before the *Sallet* is ready to be eaten: And then with the *Yolk* of two new-laid *Eggs* (boyl'd and prepar'd, as before is taught) squash, and bruise them all into mash with a Spoon; and lastly, pour it all upon the *Herbs*, stirring and mingling them 'till they are well and thoroughly imbib'd; not forgetting the Sprinklings of *Aromaticks*, and such Flowers."

Francis II Spilsbury (1733–1793) and Margaret Binley (active in London after 1764), Cruet set (with five bottles, labelled "Lemon," "Terragon," "Cayon," "Elder," "Soy"), England, London, 1770–1771. Silver and lead crystal. Royal Ontario Museum, Toronto. Gift of Norman and Marion Robertson

OPPOSITE: *Vinegar seller*, Germany, Meissen, 1753–1754. Model attributed to Peter Reinicke (1715–1768). Hard-paste porcelain, enamels, and gilding. The Alan Shimmerman Collection

Vinaigrette

Inspired by John Evelyn's recipe
Recipe by Markus Bestig, Executive Chef, The York Club, Toronto
Yields enough for the Mixed Green Salad (see pages 63–65)

INGREDIENTS

3 hard-boiled eggs, separate the yolk and the whites, and grate finely
1 tsp (5 ml) Dijon mustard
¼ cup (60 ml) red wine vinegar
1 tsp (5 ml) honey
Freshly ground black pepper
Kosher salt
¾ cup (175 ml) olive oil
1 tsp (5 ml) water

METHOD

· Finely grate the egg yolk into a bowl. Add the Dijon mustard, honey, and red wine vinegar. Season with salt and pepper. Add the olive oil in a steady stream to create a creamy emulsion. Add the water if necessary to cut the acidity.

· When it comes time to serve the prepared salad, whisk the vinaigrette to ensure it is emulsified and add little by little to just dress the salad. Too much dressing will overpower the delicate herbs and salad hearts, so taste as you go. Season lightly with salt and garnish with the reserved flowers and the grated egg whites. Serve immediately.

Salt, pepper, and mustard stand, France, Chantilly, c. 1740. Soft-paste porcelain, enamels. Private collection, Toronto

Salad bowl (*Saladier*), France, Chantilly,
c. 1740. Soft-paste porcelain, enamels.
Wadsworth Atheneum Museum of Art,
Hartford, Connecticut. Gift of Mrs.
Marion Bayard Benson

Saved by *Salad*

The young Marquis d'Albignac, who had escaped France during the Revolution with nothing more than the clothes on his back, apparently survived and prospered in England thanks to his entrepreneurial salad-making skills. The story (which may or may not be true) begins at an inn, where a group of slightly inebriated young English noblemen, who had heard of the fame of French salad, asked d'Albignac to prepare one for them. The marquis decided "to save his country's honour by making a capital salad." It was so delicious that the young men told their peers about it, and the marquis was soon invited to a grand house in Grosvenor Square in London to prepare his specialty. "He was at first greatly incensed and felt much humiliated; but he reflected that labor in any shape is more dignified than receiving alms... and resolved to make good use of the channel fortune had opened to him."[25]

The marquis quickly became famous and was known as "the Fashionable Salad-Maker." The story tells that he could soon afford to keep a carriage to get to his appointments and had a servant who followed him with a mahogany box containing all the requisites for a good salad. Not only was he able to help his fellow French exiles, but it is said he also eventually returned home with a small fortune.[26]

Pickled Cauliflower

One of the great challenges to households before the invention of canning and refrigeration was the preservation of foods for use during the winter and early spring. Pickling was one effective way of storing food, especially vegetables. Pickled vegetables became popular with the English, who relished eating them with traditional savoury pies and cheeses. Hannah Glasse (1708–1770) includes no fewer than thirty-eight recipes for pickled meat, fish, vegetables, and fruit, from walnuts to oysters, to the more unusual "pickled elder shoots in imitation of bamboo." Her readers' broadening tastes are revealed by the inclusion, in a later appendix, of a recipe for "paco-lilla, or Indian pickle," which was flavoured with turmeric, ginger, and garlic.[27]

To Pickle Cauliflowers

Hannah Glasse, *The Art of Cookery Made Plain and Easy*, 1769, 9th ed. (facsimile of 2018), pages 264–265

"Take the largest and finest you can get, cut them in little pieces, or more properly, pull them into little pieces, pick the small leaves that grow in the flowers clean from them; then have a broad stew-pan on the fire with spring-water, and when it boils, put in your flowers, with a good handful of white salt, and just let them boil up very quick; be sure you don't let them boil above one minute; then take them out with a broad slice, lay them on a cloth and cover them with another, and let them lie till they are quite cold. Then put them in your wide-mouth'd bottles with two or three blades of mace in each bottle, and a nutmeg sliced thin; then fill up your bottles with distilled vinegar, cover them over with mutton fat, over that a bladder, and then a leather. Let them stand a month before you open them.

If you find the pickle tastes sweet, as may be it will, pour off the vinegar, and put fresh in, the spice will do again. In a fortnight, they will be fit to eat. Observe to throw them out of the boiling water into cold, and then dry them."

Pickled Cauliflower

Inspired by Hannah Glasse's recipe

INGREDIENTS
1 cauliflower, approximately 4 cups (1,300 g) of florets
3 tbsp (30 g) kosher salt, divided
2 cups (500 ml) water
1 cup (250 ml) white wine vinegar, or distilled malt vinegar
4 tbsp (60 g) sugar
6 blades mace
1/2 nutmeg, coarsely grated, or thinly sliced with a mandolin
2 tsp (6 g) black peppercorns
Ice

METHOD
· Sterilize the jars: wash in the dishwasher, then place them in a preheated oven at 250 °F (120 °C) for 10 minutes. Remove and let cool.
· To prepare the pickles: rinse the cauliflower. Pull apart the florets so they are approximately the same size. Cut off excess stalks and leaves. Blanch the cauliflower: fill a large saucepan with water and 1 tbsp (10 g) of the salt; prepare a second, large saucepan or bowl with plenty of cold water and ice. Bring the first saucepan to a rolling

boil and toss in the cauliflower florets. Quickly return to a boil and cook for no more than 1 minute. Immediately remove the cauliflower with a slotted spoon and plunge into the second saucepan with the ice-cold water. If necessary, replace the cold water. When the florets are cold, remove from the pan and spread them out over a towel to dry.

· Put 2 cups (500 ml) of water in a saucepan. Add vinegar, 2 tbsp (20 g) of the salt, the sugar, and spices and bring to a boil. Simmer for 5 minutes.

· Meanwhile, pack the cold, blanched cauliflower florets into two 2-cup (500 ml) glass jars. Divide equally the hot spiced vinegar into the two jars. Fill up to ¼ in (6 mm) of the top. Loosely cover the jars and leave to cool. Once cooled, tighten the lids and refrigerate. Leave for 2 days before eating.

· Pickles will keep for at least a month when refrigerated.

Cauliflower tureen, Germany, Hannoversch-Münden, c. 1765. Tin-glazed earthenware (faïence). Private collection

Popular Pickles

The craze for pickled vegetables in England in the second half of the 1700s is illustrated by the large number of surviving porcelain pickle dishes. Most English porcelain manufacturers produced a wide variety of them, often in the shape of leaves and shells. There were even stands made for pickles or sweetmeats, with multiple containers that enabled diners to have a convenient and broad selection immediately at hand. The stand shown here was created for this purpose, as a realistic porcelain gherkin is attached to the inside of the topmost shell. No doubt it caused some confusion and merriment when the diner attempted to remove what seemed to be the last remaining pickle!

Pickle stand, England, Derby, c. 1765. Soft-paste porcelain, enamels. Gardiner Museum, Toronto. Gift of Isadore and Rosalie Sharp

Fish, Meat, AND Fowl

Crayfish in Sauternes

Fish and seafood were eaten during Lent and other days of fasting. However, methods of transporting fresh sea fish to inland towns and cities were slow and complicated and often met with little success. As a result, freshwater fish and shellfish, such as carp, trout, and crayfish, were popular choices for people who lived far from the sea. Gelatin as we now know it did not exist in the 1700s, so cooks used isinglass, a type of collagen obtained from fish bladders, or hartshorn, made from shaving the soft antlers of young male deer. They also made savoury jellies with boiled bones.

Crayfish in Savoury Jelly

Mary Smith, The Complete House-keeper, and Professed Cook, 1772, page 281

"Boil six crayfish in salt and water; when they are cold, take a bowl with a little savoury jelly, set on three crayfish with their backs down, a few sprigs of parsley, some small slices of lemon, and pour on a little jelly ... let it stand until cold, then lay in the other three crayfish, and pour in some more jelly; when cold turn it out, and garnish it with parsley."

Crayfish in Sauternes

Inspired by Mary Smith's recipe
Recipe by Markus Bestig, Executive Chef, The York Club, Toronto
Six servings

INGREDIENTS
¾ cup (175 g) finely diced root vegetables (multicoloured carrots, celery, leek)
1 tbsp (3 g) finely cut chives
1 tbsp (3 g) finely chopped parsley
1 tsp (1 g) finely chopped tarragon
1 tsp (1 g) finely chopped dill
1½ lb (680 g) 30 to 36 pieces crayfish, frozen, whole and steamed
5 sheets gold gelatin, or 10 g powdered gelatin
1 cup (250 ml) fish stock (if not available, substitute with Sauternes)
1 cup (250 ml) Sauternes wine
Kosher salt, to taste

METHOD
· Cook diced root vegetables separately in well-salted water until fully tender, there should be no crunch. Scatter onto paper towel to absorb all the moisture; veggies should be very dry. Chill fully in refrigerator. Once cold, mix in the finely cut herbs.
· The crayfish will likely be frozen and cooked, but if fresh, cook in well-salted water for 2 minutes, remove, and place into a bowl

Madame Tricot (Dominique Kähler Schweizer, b. 1948), *Crayfish*, 2019. Hand-knitted wool. Collection of the artist

and cover with plastic wrap for 5 minutes. Then peel and lay out on paper towel, reserving only the tail meat. Chill.

· Soak the sheet gelatin in very cold water for 5 minutes until it becomes jelly-like. Or, if using powdered gelatin, sprinkle over 1/2 cup (125 ml) water in a small saucepan and leave to soak.

· Bring the fish stock to a boil, squeeze all liquid out of the sheet gelatin (if used), and gently whisk in the stock until fully dissolved. Or, if using powdered gelatin, heat very gently until completely dissolved and then add to the stock. Add Sauternes and season with kosher salt to taste. Cool to room temperature, no lower, as this will trigger the gelatin to start setting.

· Place 6 small ramekins (4 oz, or 115 ml size) onto a tray for easy transport in and out of the fridge. To build the dish, pour enough jelly into each ramekin to generously cover the bottom, approximately 1/4 in (6 mm); sprinkle about 1.5 tsp (7.5 ml) of the vegetable and herb mixture and place in the fridge to just set; jelly should be soft. Into the just-set jelly, scatter more of the root vegetable and herb mix and place 3 crayfish in each ramekin, ensuring the crayfish do not touch the walls of the ramekin; sprinkle more vegetables and pour more jelly to just cover the crayfish. Let it set slightly and repeat. At the end of the process, all vegetables and crayfish should be used up. Let the jelly set in the back of the fridge for 12 hours.

· To unmould, boil some water, pour into a heat-resistant bowl, and dip the ramekins one by one for about 5 seconds. Immediately after dipping, use a sharp, fine-tipped knife to run along the side of the dish to open an air pocket at the bottom to encourage the jelly to release.

· When ready to serve, arrange some delicate salad greens and freshly picked garden herbs on 6 plates and place a jelly mould on top of each.

English *versus* French Cooks

Mary Smith is typical of many English female cookbook authors of the time, who were writing "practical" recipes "For the greater Ease of Ladies, House-keepers, Cooks, Etc." She assures her readers with her credentials: she was the "Late House-keeper to Sir Walter Blackett ... and formerly in the Service of the Right Hon. Lord Anson, Sir Tho. Sebright ... and other Families of Distinction, as House-keeper and Cook."[28] As the 1700s drew to a close, in the homes of the wealthy in England, female cooks were gradually replaced by more fashionable (and expensive) French male chefs, and French cooking began to dominate in Europe. Curiously, many cookbooks were written by English women at the time, but published French cookbooks were written solely by men. French cookbook authors included cooks (*cuisiniers*), managers of households (*maître d'hôtels*), or even garden specialists such as Nicolas de Bonnefons.

A TABLE, shewing at one View, the proper SEASONS for SEA FISH.

The ONE's signify when the FISH are in SEASON, the BLANKS when they are not.

NAMES.	Jan.	Feb.	Mar.	Ap.	May	June	July	Aug.	Sept.	Oct.	Nov.	Dec.
Brett	I	I	I	I	I	I	I	I			I	I
Bril	I	I	I	I	I					I	I	I
Cod	I	I	I	I	I						I	I
Cole-Fifh	I	I	I	I	I						I	I
Cockles	I	I	I						I	I	I	I
Crabs	I	I	I	I	I	I						
Dabbs	I	I	I	I	I	I	I	I	I			
Flounders		I	I	I	I	I	I	I				
Guarnets					I	I	I	I	I			
Haddocks	I	I								I	I	I
Herrings			I	I	I	I	I	I				
Lobfters	I	I	I	I	I					I	I	I
Ling	I	I	I	I	I	I	I				I	I
Mackrell				I	I	I	I					
Mufles	I	I	I	I						I	I	I
Oyfters									I	I	I	I
Plaice	I	I	I	I	I	I	I	I				
Salmon	I	I	I	I	I	I	I					
Soales			I	I	I	I	I					
Shrimps	I	I	I	I	I							
Sturgeon				I	I	I	I	I				
Skate	I	I	I	I	I						I	I
Thornback	I	I	I	I							I	I
Turbut				I	I	I	I	I				
Whiteings	I	I	I							I	I	I
Sea Smelt		I	I	I								
Conger Eel			I	I	I	I	I	I	I			

FISH, MEAT, AND FOWL ∞ CRAYFISH IN SAUTERNES

Chargrilled Fish with *Beurre Blanc Sauce*

François Pierre de La Varenne (1618–1678) revolutionized French cooking in the 1650s, including the preparation of fish, which he treated simply and delicately. Most frequently, he simmered it in a *court bouillon*, a broth made from white wine, herbs, and seasonings, but he also roasted fish on the grill, as featured here. Varenne's fish was sometimes served with an emulsified butter and vinegar sauce (now known as *beurre blanc*), which could be flavoured with capers and herbs. Fish was often garnished with fried parsley.

Bresme en ragoust (Ragout of Bream)

François de La Varenne, *Le vrai cuisinier françois*, 1651, page 181

"Gut it, and put a bouquet in the body, melt some butter and brush all over, & place on the grill; once roasted make a sauce with fresh butter, capers, chopped parsley and chives, simmer well with vinegar, and a little bouillon, serve once the sauce has thickened."

Chargrilled Fish with Beurre Blanc Sauce

Inspired by François de La Varenne's recipe
4 servings

INGREDIENTS
4 lb (approximately 2 kg) whole salt- or freshwater fish, such as sea bream, salmon, red snapper, sea bass, trout, or carp (allow 1 lb [approximately 450 g] per person)
2 sprigs thyme or lemon thyme
2 sprigs parsley
1/2 lemon, sliced and halved
2 tbsp (30 ml) olive or sunflower oil

For the sauce:
1 cup (225 g) butter, cold
1/2 cup (125 ml) dry white wine
1/4 cup (60 ml) white wine vinegar
2 tsp (6 g) capers, rinsed, patted dry, and chopped
2 tbsp (6 g) finely chopped parsley
2 tbsp (6 g) finely chopped or snipped chives
Kosher salt and freshly ground black pepper

METHOD
· Remove the fish from the refrigerator and allow to come to room temperature for about half an hour before cooking.
· Preheat the barbecue to medium–high. Oil the grill, or a mesh grilling basket. If using the broiler, preheat and adjust the rack so it is 4 to 5 in (10 to 13 cm) from the heat.
· First, start the sauce: cut the cold butter into cubes of about 1/2 in (13 mm) and store in the fridge. Place the wine and vinegar in a saucepan, bring to a boil, and reduce until there is about 1/2 cup (125 ml). Remove from the heat. Complete the sauce once the fish is cooked.
· To prepare the fish: rinse and scale the fish and pat very dry with paper towel. Salt and pepper the interior of the fish and stuff it with the parsley, thyme, and lemon slices. Brush the dry fish all over with oil and season the outside with more salt and freshly ground pepper.

Carp tureen and stand, England, Chelsea,
c. 1755. Soft-paste porcelain, enamels. Courtesy
of Michele Beiny

- Broil or grill the fish for about 10 minutes until lightly charred and it can be turned easily, then turn and continue to cook for another 10 minutes. Please note that the cooking time depends on the size of the fish, so check frequently. Remove and let the fish rest, covered lightly with aluminium foil, on a platter in a warm oven while finishing the sauce.
- Return the saucepan with the vinegar and wine to a light boil and reduce until 2 tbsp (30 ml) remain. Reduce heat to low and whisk in the cubes of cold butter, 2 at a time. Continue to whisk well until the sauce begins to emulsify. When only a few cubes of butter remain, remove pan from heat and whisk in the remainder. Stir in the rinsed, chopped capers and herbs. Season with salt and pepper to taste. Drizzle a little sauce over the fish and serve the rest immediately in a warm sauceboat.

The Fish That Arrived *Too Late*

In 1671, Louis II, Prince de Condé, arranged a long-awaited grand entertainment for Louis XIV and his court at his Château de Chantilly. The prince's chef, François Vatel, "a man so eminently distinguished for taste, and whose abilities were equal to the government of a state," was charged with preparing a series of great feasts in the king's honour. On the night of April 23, due to the unexpected arrival of additional guests, Vatel had been unable to provide roast meat at two tables. He declared, "I have lost my honour ... I have not had a wink of sleep these twelve nights." The following morning, in despair upon "finding ... that the fish he had sent for did not come at the time he expected it, and unable to bear the disgrace ... [Vatel] ran himself through with his own sword." Tragically, immediately after his suicide, the expected fish arrived. The Prince de Condé wept when he heard the news.[29]

Carp seller, Germany, Meissen c. 1753–1754.
Model attributed to Peter Reinicke (1715–1768).
Hard-paste porcelain, enamels, and gilding.
The Alan Shimmerman Collection

Stuffed Veal Escalopes, or "Veal Donkey Droppings Rolled in the Neuteau Style"

Le cuisinier gascon (The Gascon cook), the curious cookbook attributed to Louis-Auguste II de Bourbon, Prince de Dombes, has particularly playful titles for some of its recipes. *Poulets en culottes* (Chickens in Trousers) is the opening recipe, followed by such recipes as *Sauce au singe vert* (Green Monkey Sauce), *Caramel sans malice* (Caramel without Malice), and even *Veau en crotte d'âne roulé à la Neuteau* (Veal Donkey Droppings Rolled in the Neuteau Style). Clearly, the Prince had a sense of humour, and perhaps he invented these amusing titles to entertain his guests in a self-deprecating manner. It is possible to imagine him announcing, grandly, to his august companions at a little private dinner, "And here I present my special recipe for Rolled Donkey Droppings!"

Veau en crotte d'âne roulé à la Neuteau (Veal Donkey Droppings Rolled in the Neuteau Style)

Louis–Auguste II de Bourbon, Prince de Dombes (attributed), *Le cuisinier gascon*, 1747, pages 79–80

"Take a piece of well hung veal … cut it thinly in lengths across the grain, & make fifteen or twenty pieces, beat them well so they are the length of a hand, and two fingers' wide; once well beaten, place them on a dish, and spread on them parsley, chives, shallots, mushrooms, truffles, all well chopped, seasoned with salt and large pepper, & with oil; mix well all together and when they are tasty, roll them like small paupiettes & place them on two spits; once cooked, serve on a dish with a sauce beneath that takes your fancy, such as a green sauce, or an Italian sauce, or a shallot sauce, with clear reduction. This can be done with lamb, fillets of sirloin, rabbit and chicken: it is good."

Stuffed Veal Escalopes

Inspired by the Prince de Dombes's recipe
Could be served with Bacchus Sauce or Sauce Robert Bourgeoise
(see pages 106 and 108–109)
6 servings

INGREDIENTS
2 shallots
1¹/₂ lb (680 g) button mushrooms
1 green onion
2 large sprigs parsley
1 oz (28 g) shaved black truffle, if available, or 6 rehydrated porcini mushrooms
4 tbsp (60 ml) oil, divided
12 veal escalopes, about 4 oz (115 g) each
Kosher salt and freshly ground black pepper
Fresh lemon slices to garnish

François de Troy (1645–1730), *Louis-Auguste II de Bourbon, Prince de Dombes (1700–1755),* represented as a boy, c. 1730. Oil on canvas. Château de Versailles et de Trianon, France

OPPOSITE: Martha Bradley (dates unknown), Frontispiece showing cooks spit-roasting meat using a clockwork operated jack, *The British Housewife: or, the Cook, Housekeeper's and Gardiner's Companion,* vol. 1. London: S. Crowder and H. Woodgate, 1760. Collection of Ivan Day

METHOD
- If using wood skewers for cooking, first soak them in cold water.
- Prepare either Bacchus Sauce (without adding the herbs) or Sauce Robert Bourgeoise and set aside (see pages 106 and 108–109).
- For the stuffing: finely chop the shallots, mushrooms, green onion, parsley, and truffle or porcini mushrooms. Mix together well with 1 to 2 tbsp (15 to 30 ml) oil and season with salt and freshly ground black pepper to taste.
- Preheat the barbecue to medium and oil the grill, or preheat the broiler if using.
- Beat each of the veal escalopes until they are thin and approximately 7 in (18 cm) long × 4 in (10 cm) wide. Lightly season both sides with salt and freshly ground black pepper. Place a spoonful of stuffing on each escalope, then roll them up; fasten with a small metal trussing skewer.
- Slide the escalopes onto long wooden or metal skewers suitable for the barbecue; there should be 2 escalopes per skewer, placed separately. Lightly brush all over with oil.
- Place on the barbecue, or under the broiler, turning after 5 minutes once the meat releases from the grill; continue cooking for approximately 10 minutes longer, turning from time to time. Use a meat thermometer to check for doneness. Remove from heat when the thermometer reaches 155 °F (68 °C). Leave to rest for 10 minutes, lightly covered with foil on a warm dish; the meat will continue to cook while it rests. Do not remove the skewers.
- While resting the escalopes, complete preparations for the sauce. If using a sauce, spoon some on a warm platter, place the skewered escalopes on top, and serve, with additional sauce on the side. Or serve the escalopes with slices of lemon instead of sauce.

Plate I.   Frontispiece to the Compleat English Cook.

Jaques Le Sœur Inv.   B. Cole sc.

Behold, ye Fair, united in this Book
The frugal Housewife, and experienc'd Cook.

THE
BRITISH HOUSEWIFE:
OR, THE
COOK, HOUSEKEEPER's,
AND
GARDINER's COMPANION.
CALCULATED FOR THE
Service both of LONDON and the COUNTRY;

And directing what is neceſſary to be done in the *Providing for*, *Conducting*, and *Managing* a FAMILY throughout the Year.
CONTAINING
A general Account of freſh Proviſions of all Kinds. Of the ſeveral *foreign Articles* for the Table, pickled, or otherwiſe preſerved; and the different Kinds of *Spices, Salts, Sugars*, and other *Ingredients* uſed in *Pickling* and *Preſerving* at Home: Shewing *what each is, whence it is brought*, and what are its *Qualities* and *Uſes*.

Together with the *Nature* of all Kinds of *Foods*, and the Method of *ſuiting them to different* CONSTITUTIONS;

A BILL of FARE for each Month, the Art of *Marketing* and *chuſing* freſh Proviſions of all Kinds; and the making as well as chuſing of *Hams, Tongues*, and other *Store Diſhes*.

Alſo DIRECTIONS for plain *Roaſting* and *Boiling*; and for the Dreſſing of all Sorts of *Made Diſhes* in various Taſtes; and the preparing the *Deſert* in all its Articles.

Containing a greater Variety than was ever before publiſh'd, of the moſt Elegant, yet leaſt Expenſive RECEIPTS in

COOKERY,	FRICASSEES,	TARTS,	DRY'D FRUITS,
PASTRY,	RAGOUTS,	CAKES,	SWEETMEATS,
PUDDINGS,	SOUPS,	CREAMS,	MADE WINES,
PRESERVES,	SAUCES,	CUSTARDS,	CORDIALS, And
PICKLES,	JELLIES,	CANDIES,	DISTILLERY.

To which are annexed,
The Art of CARVING; and the Terms uſed for cutting up various Things; and the polite and eaſy Manner of *doing the Honours of the Table*: The whole Practice of *Pickling* and *Preſerving*: And of preparing *made Wines, Beer*, and *Cyder*. As alſo of *diſtilling* all the uſeful Kinds of *Cordial* and *Simple* Waters.

With the *Conduct of a Family* in Reſpect of *Health*; the *Diſorders* to which they are every *Month* liable, and the moſt approved *Remedies* for each.

And a Variety of other valuable Particulars, neceſſary to be known in *All Families*; and nothing inſerted but what has been *approved* by EXPERIENCE.

Alſo the Ordering of all Kinds of profitable *Beaſts* and *Fowls*, with reſpect to their *Choice*, their *Breeding* and *Feeding*; the *Diſeaſes* to which they are ſeverally liable each Month, and *Receipts* for their *Cure*. Together with the Management of the *pleaſant, profitable*, and *uſeful Garden*.
THE WHOLE
Embelliſhed with a great Number of *curious* COPPER PLATES, ſhewing the Manner of *Truſſing* all Kinds of GAME, wild and tame FOWLS, &c. as alſo the Order of ſetting out TABLES for *Dinners, Suppers*, and *Grand Entertainments*, in a Method never before attempted; and by which even *thoſe who cannot read* will be able to inſtruct themſelves.

By Mrs. MARTHA BRADLEY, *late of* BATH:
Being the Reſult of upwards of *Thirty Years Experience*.

The whole (which is deduc'd from *Practice*) compleating the careful Reader, from the higheſt to the loweſt Degree, in every Article of *Engliſh Houſewifery*.
LONDON:
Printed for S. *Crowder* and H. *Woodgate*, at the Golden Ball in *Paternoſter Row*.

1760

Spit-Roasting

Over the course of the 1600s and 1700s, a number of important technical advances for spit-roasting were introduced into the kitchens of prosperous families. Hearths were fitted with more efficient grates that maximized the heat and area available for roasting, while clockwork and fan-operated spits replaced hand-operated ones. To speed up roasting, cooks placed metal screens in front of the fire. These reflected the heat and sheltered the meat from drafts.[30] Kitchen workers were still responsible for the scorching job of basting roasts while they cooked, using drippings collected in a pan placed beneath the meat.

Daniel Chodowiecki (1726–1801), *The Boy with the Sausage Spit*, 1764. Etching. Los Angeles County Museum of Art, Los Angeles, California. Gift of Virgil Whirlow

Braised Beef with *Red Wine*

Despite the spread of fashionable French cuisine to most of Europe, other countries retained their regional traditions. In England, beef was king, whether it was roasted, braised, or grilled. James Boswell (1740–1795) recorded his attendance at London's famous Beefsteak Club in 1762: "The president sits in a chair under a canopy, above which you have in golden letters, *Beef and Liberty* ... Lord Sandwich was in the chair, a jolly, hearty, lively man ... We had nothing to eat but beefsteaks, and had wine and punch in plenty and freedom. We had a number of songs."[31] Boswell notes that chophouses also provided beef, bread, and beer for just a shilling.[32]

To Stew a Rump of Beef

Elizabeth Raffald, *The Experienced English Housekeeper*, 1769, page 114

"Half roast your Beef, then put it in a large Sauce Pan or Caldron, with two Quarts of Water and one of Red Wine, two or three Blades of Mace, a Shallot, one Spoonful of Lemon Pickle, two of Walnut Catchup, the same of Browning, Chyan Pepper and Salt to your Taste, let it stew over a gentle Fire, close covered for two Hours, then take up your Beef, and lay it in a deep Dish, skim off the Fat, and strain the Gravy, and put in one Ounce of Morels, and half a Pint of Mushrooms, thicken your Gravy and pour it over your Beef, lay around it Force-Meat Balls: garnish with Horseradish and serve up."

Braised Beef with Red Wine

Inspired by Elizabeth Raffald's recipe
4 to 6 servings

INGREDIENTS
2¾ lb (1.25 kg) beef chuck for pot roasting (in a single large piece)
1 tbsp (15 ml) oil
8 large shallots, whole and peeled
1 cup (250 ml) red wine
½ cup (125 ml) beef stock (may be made from concentrate)
3 tbsp (45 ml) Worcestershire sauce
1 bay leaf
Kosher salt and freshly ground black pepper
1 oz (28 g) morels, optional
8 oz (227 g) button mushrooms, optional
1 tbsp (15 g) butter, optional
Easy-mixing or instant-blend flour, or 1 generous tbsp (10 g) all-purpose flour mixed with 1 tbsp (15 g) soft butter

METHOD
- Preheat oven to 275 °F (135 °C).
- Pat the meat dry with paper towel, then lightly season with salt and freshly ground black pepper.
- Heat the oil in a large frying pan. When very hot, put in the meat; turn when well browned on one side and not sticking to the surface of the pan. Add the shallots and brown. Remove the meat and the shallots and place in a casserole, arranging the meat so it fits on one level; cut to fit if necessary. Scatter the shallots at random.
- Discard the oil from the frying pan and deglaze with the red wine and stock; scrape to remove any brown crusty residue from the bottom of the pan. Add the Worcestershire sauce. Pour the heated mixture over the meat and add the bay leaf. The meat should just be covered by the liquid. Heat gently on the stove to just boiling, then place casserole in the oven and cook for 3 hours. Check each hour; stir and baste if necessary. The liquid should be simmering or boiling very gently. If it is boiling steadily, lower the heat.
- Optional: meanwhile, slice the morels and mushrooms, fry them gently in butter, and season well with salt and freshly ground black pepper.
- When the beef is cooked (it should be very tender), remove it from the casserole with the shallots and place them on a large dish. Discard the bay leaf and lemon rind. Cover the meat and shallots with foil to keep warm.
- Skim the fat from the surface of the liquid in the casserole by using several sheets of paper towel laid gently on the surface and then removed. Replace the casserole on the stove and heat at medium-low. Thicken the sauce with lightly shaken easy-blend flour, whisking constantly and adding more flour, until the mixture boils and the desired thickness is achieved. Alternatively, thicken by adding the kneaded butter and flour little by little to the hot sauce, whisking constantly until the mixture boils and thickens. If desired, add the cooked mushrooms and any juices to the sauce. Replace the meat and the shallots in the casserole, reheat gently, and serve.

Note: if only 2 or 3 servings are taken from the cooked braised beef, there will be enough left over for the Thatched House Pie (see pages 89–92).

Jean-Baptiste de Roy (1759–1839), *Landscape with Cattle and Cottage*, 1796. Oil on panel. Wadsworth Atheneum Museum of Art, Hartford, Connecticut. Gift of Mr. and Mrs. James Lippincott Goodwin

OPPOSITE: Plate with pastoral scene, France, Marseilles, 1750–1800. Tin-glazed earthenware (faïence). Gardiner Museum, Toronto. The Pierre Karch and Mariel O'Neill-Karch Collection

Animal Husbandry

In England, the 1700s was a period of agricultural reform and advancement. Changes in farming and animal husbandry made fresh meat available year-round to those who could afford it. More crops such as turnips and grasses were grown to provide winter food for animals. Experiments in breeding livestock and their careful feeding by pioneers such as Robert Bakewell led to the development of much larger animals with superior quality meat.[33] In both England and France, the poor seldom ate meat, though records show that diets gradually improved, and by the 1780s most people in Paris sometimes were eating meat or eggs.[34] Famine continued to be widespread, however. The failure of grain crops in 1788 and 1789 resulted in bread riots in Paris, a contributing factor of the French Revolution.

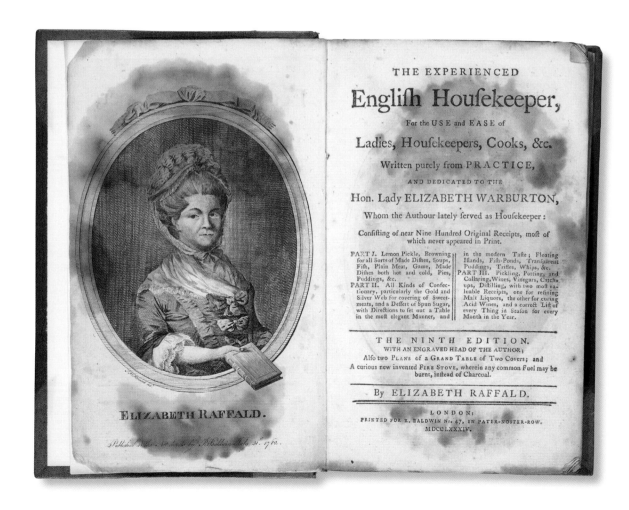

Elizabeth Raffald (1733–1781), Title page and frontispiece with a portrait of the author, *The Experienced English Housekeeper, For the use and ease of Ladies, Housekeepers, Cooks, &c.*, 9th ed. London: Printed for R. Baldwin, 1784. Thomas Fisher Rare Book Library, University of Toronto

Thatched House Pie

Although savoury pies are found in most European cookbooks, they are a particular feature of English cooking. Pigeon pie was one of the most popular of all English pies, so it is not surprising that Elizabeth Raffald, the author of this curious pie recipe, calls for it to be filled with "three or four" pigeons. She also states in *The Experienced English Housekeeper* that it would be ideal as a "pretty side or corner dish for a large dinner, or a bottom for a supper." Another English cook, Martha Bradley, illustrates a pigeon pie in her plan for *A Dinner for December, First Course* (see page 92). Because pigeons for consumption are not widely available, the filling of this pie has been replaced with beef.

Thatched House Pye

Elizabeth Raffald, *The Experienced English Housekeeper*, 1769, page 131–132

"Take an Earthen Dish that is pretty deep, rub the inside with two Ounces of Butter, then spread over it two Ounces of Vermicelli, make a good puff Paste, and roll it out pretty thick, and lay it on the Dish; take three or four Pigeons, season them well with Pepper and Salt, and put a good Lump of Butter in them, and lay them in the Dish with the Breast down, and put a thick Lid over them, and bake it in a moderate Oven; when enough, take the Dish you intend for it, and turn the Pye on to it, and the Vermicelli will appear like Thatch, which gives it the name of Thatched House Pye. It is a pretty side or corner dish for a large dinner, or a bottom for a supper."

Thatched House Pie

Inspired by Elizabeth Raffald's recipe
If you are starting from scratch with the beef, make ⅔ of the Braised Beef with Red Wine recipe the day before.
4 generous servings

INGREDIENTS
2 sheets frozen puff pastry, 10 × 10 in (25 × 25 cm), defrosted
1½ to 2 oz (42.5 to 60 g) straight vermicelli pasta, uncooked
2 tbsp (30 g) soft butter
3 cups (700 ml) leftover Braised Beef with Red Wine (see pages 85–86)

If more gravy is needed:
2 tsp (10 g) butter
3 shallots, peeled and cut in half
2 tsp (6 g) flour
¼ cup (60 ml) beef stock
¼ cup (60 ml) red wine
Salt and freshly ground black pepper

METHOD

- Preheat oven to 425 °F (215 °C).
- Very generously butter the bottom of a large oval or circular pie dish; lightly butter the sides and edge of the dish. Break up the vermicelli and place a layer in the bottom; if possible, divide it in half in the middle to resemble the peak of a roof.
- Roll out the first sheet of pastry on a lightly floured surface until it is about 1/4 in (6 mm) or less thick. Roll it over the rolling pin and place carefully in the pie dish on top of the vermicelli. Leave about 1 inch (2.5 cm) of pastry hanging over the edge. Put the pie dish in the refrigerator to chill for at least half an hour.
- Remove the pie dish and prick the base and sides of the pastry a few times with a fork. Cut a large piece of parchment paper that will fit the interior of your dish with enough to rise a good inch (2.5 cm) above the edge. Place the paper in the dish and fill at least halfway with beans or rice. Bake for about 15 minutes (check after 12 minutes) until the edge is just beginning to turn golden and remove from the oven. Remove the parchment and the beans or rice and return the pie dish to the oven for 5 minutes.
- Remove the pie dish and place on a rack. Let it cool for no more than 5 minutes, then using scissors or a sharp knife, trim the pastry while it is still warm, so it is flush with the outer edge of the pie dish. Use a flat knife to gently ease the pastry from the edge. Leave to cool.
- While the pastry is baking: cut the beef into bite-size pieces and assess how much gravy you have if using leftovers. To prepare more gravy: melt the butter in a small saucepan, add the shallots, and cook until they are brown on one side. Turn and continue to cook for 1 or 2 minutes. Shake in the flour, stir until it is combined and has had a chance to cook a little. Mix the stock and wine together and pour it in, whisking or stirring until it is all combined to make a thick sauce. Season with salt and pepper to taste and place in the fridge to cool.
- When cool, add the additional shallots and sauce to the leftover beef and gravy and stir together. Then spoon all the cold beef, shallots (and mushrooms, if used), and gravy into the pie dish.
- Roll out the second piece of pastry for the top crust on a lightly floured surface until it is between 1/8 and 1/4 in (3 and 6 mm) thick. Roll the pastry onto the rolling pin and carefully place on top of the pie. Cut around the edge so there is about 1/2 to 3/4 in (13 to 19 mm) overhang all around the edge of the pie. Now tuck the overhang underneath the outside edge of the pre-baked pastry, little by little, as best you can. It will not be perfect, but just ensure you have a rolled edge around the pastry dish. Use a fork to crimp the edges.
- Cut 3 small vents in the top of the pie and place in the oven for about 60 minutes. Check after 45 minutes. Test with a meat thermometer to see if the meat is hot: 160 °F (70 °C). If necessary, cover the edges of the dish with a ring of aluminium foil, to prevent over-browning during the last 15 minutes of cooking. The pie should be done when the top crust is a medium golden brown.
- Once cooked, use a flat knife to ease the crust from around the edge. Place over the top a dish large enough to hold the inverted pie and flip over the baked pie, removing the pie dish to show the "thatched" roof. If necessary, place the dish under the broiler for a few minutes until the vermicelli is browned. Note: the thatch may more accurately resemble a bird's nest!

Pair of pigeon tureens, France, Strasbourg, c. 1748.
Model by Johann Wilhelm Lanz (active 1748–1761).
Tin–glazed earthenware (faïence). Museum of Fine
Arts, Boston, Massachusetts. The Kiyi and Edward
M. Pflueger Collection. Bequest of Edward
M. Pflueger and Gift of Kiyi Powers Pflueger

Vermicelli and Other Pastas

Unlike many cookbook authors of the period, Elizabeth Raffald did not copy recipes from other writers, preferring to use her own for both savoury and sweet dishes. Her Thatched House Pye is both imaginative and original; the thatch is cleverly imitated with imported vermicelli. A variety of dried pastas was exported from Italy all over Europe in the 1700s. Another writer, Mrs. Pennington, author of *The Royal Cook*, includes both macaroni and vermicelli on her list of essential ingredients to bring from London to the country during the summer. Ravioli, macaroni with milk and cheese, and a form of lasagna are among the recipes of the Prince de Dombes in *Le cuisinier gascon* (The Gascon cook), but his pastas were all freshly made.[35]

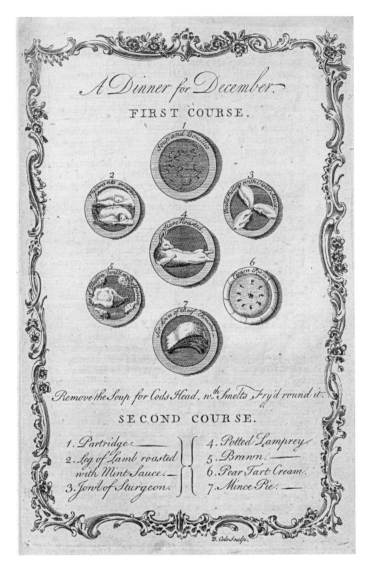

Necessary Things to be provided when a Family is going into the Country for a Summer.

Nutmegs, cinnamon, cloves, mace, pepper, ginger, Jamaica pepper, currants, raisins, sugar, Lisbon, sugar loaf, lump, sugar double-refined, prunes, oranges, lemons, anchovies, olives, capers, mangoes, oil for sallads, vinegar, verjuice, tea, coffee, chocolate, almonds, chesnuts, French pears, sagoe, truffles, morels, macroni, vermicelli, rice, millet, comfits, and pistachoe nuts.

Mrs. Pennington (dates unknown), Necessary Things to be provided when a Family is going into the Country for a Summer, *The Royal Cook; or, the Modern Etiquette of the Table, displayed with Accuracy, Elegance, and Taste.* London: Richard Snagg, 1774. Harvard University, Schlesinger Library on the History of Women in America, Cambridge, Massachusetts

Martha Bradley (dates unknown), A Dinner for December, First Course, *The British Housewife: or, the Cook, Housekeeper's and Gardiner's Companion*, vol. 2. London: S. Crowder and H. Woodgate, 1760. Collection of Ivan Day

Chicken Fricassee with Cream and Mushrooms

An obsession with white food in the 1700s may account for the popularity of fricassees made with cream-based sauces. Cooks usually prepared fricassees on one of the new stoves, called *potagers* in French, built of bricks with open hobs heated from underneath by hot cinders. They enabled greater control of heat, which was necessary when cooking fashionable sauces and dishes enriched with cream or eggs.[36] Fricassees could be kept hot on the dining table on a small brazier, or in a covered dish heated by a lamp underneath.

Fricassée de poulets à la crème aux mousserons (Chicken Fricassee with Cream and Mousseron Mushrooms)

François Marin, *Suite des dons de Comus*, vol. 2, 1742, pages 147–148

"Take two small pullets ... and put them in a casserole with a bouquet garni, mousserons, salt, two pats of butter. Simmer them on hot cinders. The juice from the mushrooms, the butter and the juice from the chickens will be enough to cook them. To finish, put in a *demi-septier* [approximately half a pint, or one cup] of good cream, and half a pat of kneaded butter. Nothing acidic." Marin also notes, "In general, a fricassee is only as good as it is simple."

Chicken Fricassee with Cream and Mushrooms

Recipe inspired by Marin's recipe
4 servings

INGREDIENTS
1 small chicken, preferably grain fed and organic, or 4 chicken quarters
4 tbsp (60 g) butter, divided
1 cup (75 g) mousseron mushrooms, or a mixture of other mushrooms such as morels, chanterelles, oyster mushrooms, or baby portabellas, cleaned and sliced in half, or left whole if small
1½ lb (680 g) button mushrooms, cleaned and cut in half, or left whole if small
Bouquet garni made of 3 large sprigs each of thyme, parsley, and marjoram, and a bay leaf, tied together with string
½ cup (125 ml) dry white wine (if desired)
1 tbsp (10 g) all-purpose flour
1 cup (250 ml) whipping or double cream
Kneaded butter made with 2 tbsp (30 g) soft butter and 2 tbsp (20 g) all-purpose flour
Kosher salt and freshly ground pepper
Finely chopped parsley to garnish
Slices of fresh lemon to garnish

METHOD

- Rinse and pat dry the chicken and cut into four quarters, removing the breast- and backbones. Pat dry again. Season well all over with salt and freshly ground black pepper.
- Melt 2 tbsp (30 g) of the butter in a casserole over a medium-high heat; when the butter is golden brown, place the chicken pieces in, skin side down, and brown all over. If necessary, fry the chicken pieces two at a time, so they are not overcrowded in the casserole. Once browned, remove the chicken and add the mushrooms; add a little additional butter if necessary. Stir and cook for a few minutes. Lower the heat to a gentle simmer, replace the chicken, add the bouquet garni, and cover tightly. Simmer very gently for 20 to 30 minutes until the chicken is tender and the mushrooms are cooked. Check while simmering; if the casserole is too dry, add ½ cup (125 ml) white wine. Remove the cooked chicken, and then the mushrooms with a slotted spoon; keep them warm. Remove and discard the bouquet garni.
- To prepare the sauce: first remove any excess fat from the surface of the remaining liquid with a sheet or two of paper towel placed gently on top and removed. Add the cream to the casserole, stirring continuously; heat gently but do not boil. Next add the kneaded butter a little at a time (you may not require it all) and simmer gently until the sauce thickens. Season to taste with salt and freshly ground pepper and replace the chicken.
- Serve garnished with a sprinkling of finely chopped parsley and slices of lemon.

Sebastian Crespel I (active 1760–1799), Dish and cover with stand and lamp, England, London, 1772–1773. Silver with wooden knob. The Sterling and Francine Clark Art Institute, Williamstown, Massachusetts. Acquired by Sterling and Francine Clark, 1930

Chickens at *Versailles* and in *Paris*

In 1749 and 1751, René Antoine Ferchault de Réaumur published scientific treatises on raising domestic fowl, and breeding chickens became a popular pastime with some princes. Among them was Louis XV, who raised chickens in the attics at Versailles.[37] Later, Queen Marie Antoinette had a special henhouse among her farm buildings at the idyllic Hameau at Versailles.[38]

When Giacomo Casanova visited France in 1758–1759, he rented a house on the outskirts of Paris, where he entertained lavishly. "Everyone talked of the excellent table I kept. I had fowl fed on rice in a dark room; they were white as snow, with an exquisite flavour. To the excellence of French cuisine, I offered whatever the other cuisines of Europe offered to tempt the most refined palates ... I matched well-chosen guests with exquisite suppers, at which my company saw that my pleasure depended on the pleasure I provided for them."[39]

Cockerel tureen, Portugal, Real Fábrica de Louça do Rato, c. 1765. Tin-glazed earthenware (faïence). Private collection

Duck with *Bitter Orange Sauce*

A wide variety of birds were consumed as food in the 1700s. Some, as now, were raised domestically, such as chickens, geese, ducks, pigeons, and turkeys. Others were hunted or snared in the wild: from quails, pheasants, partridge, grouse, woodcocks, and snipe to waterfowl such as wild ducks, plovers, and teals. Even small songbirds were relished, such as robins, sparrows, and ortolans. In place of Menon's duck from Rouen, where the best French ducks were raised, the transformed recipe by Markus Bestig calls for Brome Lake duck, a famous product of Québec.

Canetons de Roüen à la broche (Spit-Roasted Ducks from Rouen)

Menon (attrib.), *The Art of Modern Cookery Displayed*, 1767, page 238

"If you would have it for a First-course Dish, give it a few Turns with Butter in a Stew-pan over the Fire, wrap it in Paper to roast; it must not be too much done; serve with a good Consumee Sauce, chopt Shallots, the Juice of an Orange, Pepper and Salt; if for a Second-course Dish, roast it without Paper crisp: also serve with Juice of Seville Orange."

Sauce au jus d'orange (Orange Juice Sauce)

Menon, *La cuisiniere bourgeoise*, 1756, vol. 2, page 252

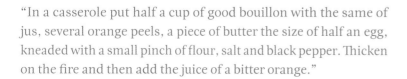

"In a casserole put half a cup of good bouillon with the same of jus, several orange peels, a piece of butter the size of half an egg, kneaded with a small pinch of flour, salt and black pepper. Thicken on the fire and then add the juice of a bitter orange."

Brome Lake Duck with Bitter Orange Sauce

Inspired by Menon's recipes
Recipe by Markus Bestig, Executive Chef, The York Club, Toronto
6 servings

INGREDIENTS

For the sauce:
2 tbsp (30 ml) vegetable oil, or rendered duck fat
1 tbsp (6 g) ginger, minced
2 tbsp (20 g) shallot, minced
5 cloves garlic, crushed separately
5 black peppercorns
1 tsp (2 g) coriander seeds
1 lb (450 g) roasted duck bones
½ cup (125 ml) orange brandy, such as Grand Marnier or Cointreau
½ cup (125 ml) brandy
2 oranges, juiced, and zest of 1 orange, peeled with sharp peeler
1 bay leaf
1 in (2.5 cm) stick of cinnamon
4 cups (950 ml) chicken stock, no sodium, preferably homemade

For the roux:
1 tbsp (15 ml) rendered duck fat
2 tbsp (20 g) all-purpose flour
1 generous tbsp (15 ml) bitter orange marmalade
1 lemon, juiced

For the duck:

6 approximately 14 oz (400 g) Brome Lake duck
  breasts
5 sprigs thyme
1 sprig rosemary
Ground black pepper as needed
Kosher salt as needed
1 tbsp (15 g) unsalted butter (if using oven method)

METHOD

· To prepare the sauce: start the sauce by heating
  1 tbsp (15 ml) of the oil, or duck fat, on a medium
  heat; add the ginger to colour a little, then add
  shallots, 2 of the crushed garlic cloves, and the
  spices and sauté to a golden colour.
· Add the duck bones and deglaze the pan with
  ¼ cup (60 ml) of the orange brandy and all the
  brandy (be careful if using open flame): pull
  the pot away, carefully add the liqueur, and
  flambé.
· Reduce the alcohol by half; once the flame has
  extinguished itself, add ¾ of the orange juice,
  the bay leaf, cinnamon stick, two sprigs of the
  thyme, half the rosemary, and the chicken stock.
· Reduce this stock on a low to medium flame by
  approximately half. Make sure to continuously

Maria Sibylla Merian (1647–1717), Atlas moths
feeding on *Citrus aurantium* (Bitter orange),
Metamorphosis insectorum Surinamensium.
Amsterdam, Voor den auteur ..., als ook by Gerarde
Valck, 1705. Hand-coloured engraving. Natural
History Museum, London, UK

skim any impurities that come to the top as they may impart an undesirable flavour. Taste as the stock reduces; if the cinnamon flavour gets too strong, remove the cinnamon stick. Once reduced by half, add the orange peel and let steep for 15 minutes. Strain this stock through a fine mesh strainer. Let it cool.

· To prepare the roux: in a separate pot over a medium heat, melt down the rendered duck fat and add the flour, continuously stirring with a wooden spoon, until the flour has reached a blonde colour. The longer the flour cooks, the less thickening strength it will have, but it will impart a nuttier flavour. Add the reduced stock and whisk until it boils, watching especially the bottom of the pot as the flour may start to stick and burn. Reduce heat to a light simmer and cook for approximately 5 minutes. Pass this sauce again through a fine mesh strainer.

· To finish the sauce: bring the bitter orange marmalade and the rest of the orange brandy to a boil; add the thickened sauce and bring to a second boil, stirring as you go to avoid burning. Mix equal parts lemon juice and the rest of the orange juice (reserve 1 tbsp [15ml] of mixed juice for later use with the duck). Stir in the juice mixture to the sauce and adjust the sweetness. The sauce should be more savoury than sweet. Season with salt and freshly ground pepper.

· To prepare the duck: crush 3 of the garlic cloves, 3 sprigs of thyme, and half the rosemary to release the oils and massage this into the duck breasts; season with pepper and chill for approximately 1 hour.

· Set the sous-vide machine, if using, to 136.4 °F (58 °C). Season the duck breasts with salt and sear the skin side in a medium-hot pan that is lightly oiled. Sear until golden brown, for approximately 3 minutes, add crushed garlic, and cook for another minute. Let cool slightly and vacuum seal with the 3 sprigs of thyme and half the rosemary in a bag, or use a Ziploc bag with the air displaced. Cook for 90 minutes.

· Remove the duck from bag and sear the skin side again in a lightly oiled pan to achieve ultimate crispiness; kiss the meat side in the hot pan for approximately 30 seconds. Slice and sprinkle with the lemon and orange juice mixture, then serve.

· If you are not using the sous-vide technique, preheat the oven to 450 °F (235 °C) and sear the breasts as above until a golden colour is achieved, approximately 5 to 10 minutes. Add the remaining thyme and rosemary to the pan and roast skin side down in the oven for 10 minutes with the butter. Remove pan from oven and remove meat from the pan. Rest skin side up for approximately 4 to 5 minutes.

· Slice the duck breasts and sprinkle with the reserved 1 tbsp (15 ml) of mixed juices. Garnish the dish with any remaining herbs. Present the remaining sauce separately and serve immediately.

Duck and duckling tureen, Belgium, Brussels, c.1750. Tin-glazed earthenware (faïence). Courtesy of Michele Beiny

Quintessences and Bitter Oranges

Markus Bestig's recipe involves a complex stock in homage to the *quintessence* and *jus* reductions favoured by mid-1700s cooks Marin and Menon, who transformed French cuisine. *Quintessences* and *jus* were intense reductions of meat and vegetable stocks that could be added by the spoonful to give depth of flavour to recipes. Cooks and diners considered them to be good for health. Little porcelain *pots à jus* were sometimes placed on the table so diners could consume these reductions separately or adjust the taste of a dish themselves.

Menon's recipe for orange sauce calls for the juice and peel of a bitter orange (*citrus aurantium*), also known as a Seville orange and now used mainly for marmalade. Bitter orange was a favourite acidic component of many recipes from the 1600s and 1700s.

Pot à jus (or pot à crème), Belgium, Tournai, c. 1765–1770. Soft-paste porcelain, enamels, and gilding. Gardiner Museum, Toronto. The Hans Syz Collection

Cook, Germany, Meissen, c. 1753–1754. Model attributed to Peter Reinicke (1715–1768). Hard-paste porcelain, enamels, and gilding. The Alan Shimmerman Collection

Roast Turkey with *Chestnut Stuffing*

The Spanish introduced turkeys to Europe from Mexico as early as the 1500s, and they gradually became popular with both cooks and diners. Louis XIV had turkeys raised at Versailles in his menagerie. He appointed a keeper with the grand title of Captain of the Royal Turkeys, who was responsible for their care.[40]

To Roast a Fowl with Chestnuts

Hannah Glasse, *The Art of Cookery Made Plain and Easy*, 1769, 9th ed. (facsimile of 2018), page 72

"First take some chestnuts, roast them very carefully, so as not to burn them, take off the skin, and peel them, take about a dozen of them cut small, and bruise them in a mortar; parboil the liver of the fowl, bruise it, and cut a quarter of a pound of ham or bacon, and pound it; then mix them all together, with a good deal of parsley chopped small, a little sweet-herbs, some mace, pepper, salt, and nutmeg; mix these together and put into your fowl, and roast it. The best way of doing it is to tie the neck, and hang it by the legs to roast with a string, and baste it with butter. For sauce take the rest of the chestnuts peeled and skinned, put them in some good gravy, with a little white wine, and thicken it with a piece of butter rolled in flour: then take up your fowl, lay it in the dish, and pour in the sauce. Garnish with lemon."

Andrew Fogelberg (active 1773–1793), Argyle (gravy warmer), England, London, 1777–1778. Silver and wood. Wadsworth Atheneum Museum of Art, Hartford, Connecticut. The Elizabeth B. Miles Collection of English Silver

Roast Turkey with Chestnut Stuffing and Gravy

Inspired by Hannah Glasse's recipe
6 to 8 servings (or 6 with leftovers)

INGREDIENTS

For the turkey:
1 10 lb (4.5 kg) turkey (liver and giblets removed and reserved)
1 peeled medium onion, halved
Several sprigs parsley, thyme, and marjoram
1 tsp (2 g) ground nutmeg
4 to 5 tbsp (60 to 75 g) soft butter
Kosher salt and freshly ground pepper

For the stuffing:
7 oz (200 g) vacuum-packed whole cooked chestnuts (divided, retain 6 for gravy)
8 rashers smoked bacon
Butter, if required
Liver from the turkey
1 large onion, chopped, or two medium onions
4 cups (200 g) fresh soft bread crumbs, or cubed soft white bread
4 tbsp (12 g) fresh parsley, chopped
3 tbsp (9 g) mixed, chopped fresh thyme and marjoram
1/2 tsp (1 g) poultry seasoning
1/4 tsp (1 g) grated nutmeg
2/3 cup (160 ml) chicken stock
Kosher salt and ground black pepper
Butter for greasing the Bundt tin

For the gravy:
6 remaining chestnuts, pounded in a mortar
3 cups (700 ml) good chicken stock, hot
1/2 cup (125 ml) dry white wine
3 to 4 tbsp (30 to 40 g) instant-blend flour
Kosher salt and ground black pepper

METHOD

- Remove the turkey from the fridge 2 hours before cooking; remove all packaging, the giblets, and liver. Leave the turkey out to reach room temperature. Refrigerate the giblets and liver until used.
- To prepare the stuffing: preheat oven to 350 °F (175 °C). Butter a Bundt tin, or a 9 × 9 in (23 × 23 cm) ovenproof glass or metal pan. Rinse and chop the chestnuts and put aside. Fry 8 rashers of bacon until crisp and put aside. Take 1/3 cup (80 ml) of the bacon drippings (if not enough, add some melted butter) and fry the turkey liver until just cooked; remove and also put aside. Add the onion to the frying pan and fry until soft and a little brown; add the chopped chestnuts. Chop the bacon and liver separately. Transfer the onion mixture, the bacon, and the liver to a large bowl and toss lightly with the bread crumbs, the herbs, the nutmeg, and salt and freshly ground pepper to taste, adding additional bread crumbs, or cubes of bread, if necessary. Pour over the stock. Adjust seasoning. Place the stuffing in the Bundt tin, or other ovenproof container. Bake in the oven for 55 to 60 minutes until the top is crisp and lightly brown (this can be done while the turkey is resting prior to carving). Invert the Bundt tin over a platter before serving.
- To prepare the turkey: preheat oven to 325 °F (165 °C). Rinse the turkey all over with cold running water; pat dry inside and out with a paper towel. Check for and remove any remaining feathers or quills. Season inside cavity with salt and pepper. Place the onion and herbs in the cavity. Truss the turkey so the legs are tied together and the wings are close to the body. Lavishly butter the breasts, legs, and wings and season well with salt and pepper. Cover with foil. Increase oven temperature to 425 °F (215 °C). Cook for 2 hours. Remove foil, baste, and cook for a further 20 minutes, or until meat thermometer inserted into thigh or breast registers 150 °F (65 °C) and the skin is a deep golden brown. Remove, cover lightly with foil, and let the turkey rest for 45 to 60 minutes; it will continue to cook as it rests.

· To prepare the gravy: skim most of the fat from the surface of the pan, leaving some fat and all the juices and crusty bits. Boil down until a generous 1/2 to 2/3 cup (125 to 160 ml) remains. Shake on the instant-blend flour, little by little, whisking continuously, and let the roux cook gently for 1 to 2 minutes. Whisk in the hot stock and the wine, bringing slowly to a boil, when the gravy will thicken. Simmer gently, add the pounded chestnuts, and stir. If the gravy is too thick, add a little hot water. Season to taste with kosher salt and freshly ground black pepper. Keep warm until served.

Turkey tureen, Germany, Höchst, c. 1760. Probably decorated by Johannes Zeschinger (b. 1723). Tin-glazed earthenware (faïence). Courtesy of Michele Beiny

The *Agonies* of Carving Turkey

Etiquette demanded that gentlemen be familiar with the art of carving. To help, books of instructions with diagrams showed how to carve every possible type of flesh, with each one requiring specialized knowledge. De La Varenne's (1618–1678) instructions on carving a *coq d'Inde* (turkey) included sixteen specific cuts, and he noted that a turkey could be carved on a dish, or on a fork in the air! The *coq d'Inde* was the name in French then given to the turkey; it is now shortened to *dinde* or *dindon*. Between 1744 and 1745, the young and painfully self-conscious Giacomo Casanova was in Corfu, working as an adjunct to the commander of the Venetian fleet. One evening, he was instructed to carve a turkey for the assembled diners. Casanova hacked the turkey into six pieces, and "Signora F., who could not supress her laughter, looked at me and said that since I was not sure I could carve it properly, I should have let it alone. Not knowing what to answer, I blushed, I sat down, I hated her."[41]

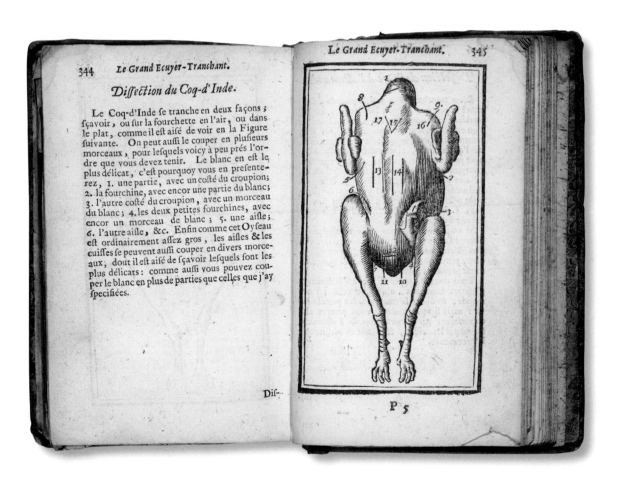

François de La Varenne (1618–1678), Dissection du Coq d'Inde, *Le Vray Cuisinier François* (*Le Grand Ecuyer-Tranchant*), new ed. Brussels: G. de Backer, 1729. Thomas Fisher Rare Book Library, University of Toronto

Sauces

Bacchus Sauce & Cold Ravigote Sauce

The sauces in the next four recipes are typical of the refined, healthy cooking advocated by François Marin and his compatriot Menon. They use carefully selected fresh ingredients combined with excellent technique to create a well-balanced dish. Mr. B. Clermont, who translated *Les soupers de la cour, où la cuisine reformée* in 1767, added his own notes to sections of the cookbook. He gives specific instructions to his English readers who are attempting to make French sauces: "This is where true Taste shows itself, and must meet with Approbation or Condemnation; as all boiled Meats stewed or brazed are to be made relishing, with the Addition of a well-timed good Sauce, and as it is absolutely impossible to direct Quantities so minutely as to agree with different Palates, I shall strongly recommend to all Cooks of either Sex, to keep their Stomach free from strong Liquors, and Noses from Snuffs."[42]

Sauce bachique qui peut servir de sauce verte & picante (Bacchus Sauce that can be used as a green & picante sauce)

Menon, *La cuisiniere bourgeoise*, 1756, vol. 2, pages 260–261

"Put a spoon of fine oil in a casserole, a *demi-septier* of good bouillon, a *chopine* of white wine, boil together and reduce by more than half, then add shallot, watercress, tarragon, chervil, parsley, green onion, a little garlic, all chopped very finely, salt, black pepper; boil it all together for a moment and then serve."

Bacchus Sauce

Inspired by Menon's recipe
Perfect for serving with roast lamb

INGREDIENTS
½ cup (125 ml) strong homemade beef stock, or consommé
2 cups (500 ml) dry white wine
1 small clove garlic, minced
1 shallot, minced
1 tbsp (15 g) butter
½ cup (12 g) in total fresh watercress, tarragon, parsley, chervil, green onion in equal quantities, all chopped together
Kosher salt and freshly ground black pepper

METHOD
· Reduce the stock and wine together by more than half in a saucepan over a medium-high heat. Add minced garlic and shallot and swirl in the butter; cook for a few minutes. Then add all the herbs and seasoning. Bring quickly to a boil and serve immediately.

Ravigotte froide (Cold Ravigote Sauce)

François Marin, *Les dons de Comus*, 1739, page 163

"Take a pinch of pimpernel, tarragon, chervil, and an equal amount of these herbs depending on their strength, a little balm, the green part of a spring onion, all well chopped and cut up; thin with oil, vinegar, mustard, salt and pepper." (An alternative recipe given by Marin calls for an anchovy, a clove of garlic, and a shallot as well.)

Cold Ravigote Sauce

Inspired by Marin's recipe
May be served over cold salmon or chicken; a salad made of fresh tomatoes;
    artichokes, or other cold vegetables

INGREDIENTS
4 large sprigs parsley or chervil
An equal amount of a selection of three of the following fresh herbs:
    tarragon, oregano, rosemary, marjoram, or basil
1 green onion
¼ cup (60 ml) red wine vinegar
1 tsp (5 ml) Dijon mustard
¾ cup (175 ml) extra virgin olive oil
Kosher salt and freshly ground black pepper

METHOD
· Remove the stalks from the herbs and mince finely; thinly slice the green parts of the spring onion and reserve. Combine the vinegar and mustard, a pinch of salt, and freshly ground pepper and add the oil while whisking to combine. Stir in the fresh herbs. Taste and adjust the seasoning. Drizzle over cold fish or chicken, or vegetable salads.

The Fashion for Sauces

Perhaps more than anything, it was sauces that defined French cooking. By the 1750s, when French cookbooks appeared in English translation and French cooking was becoming fashionable, English silversmiths and porcelain manufacturers started production of an extraordinary variety of sauceboats. They must have been a response to demand reflecting a change in the way that food was eaten. Even Hannah Glasse (1708–1770), who so despised extravagant French cooking, had sauces to accompany most meats. She also called for melted butter to be poured over fish and many vegetables and frequently instructed that it and other sauces were to be served in cups or boats.[43]

Simon Le Sage (born c. 1739), Sauceboat, England, London, 1760–1761. Silver. Royal Ontario Museum. Bequest of Gerald R. Larkin

Onion Sauce *Robert Bourgeoise* & Chervil or *Parsley Sauce* for Chicken

There were a variety of ways to thicken sauces. In the 1650s, La Varenne used egg yolks mixed with *bouillon* (clear broth or stock), verjuice, or cream as a thickener for some sauces and ragouts, as well as an emulsion made of butter added slowly to a reduction of vinegar or another acid.[44] Additional ways of thickening sauces were developed a little later. They included deglazed sauces with the addition of butter; *roux* made of butter and flour; and *beurre manié*, a paste of soft butter kneaded with flour, which was incorporated gradually at the end of cooking. Alternatively, sauces could be thickened simply by reduction, or by puréeing vegetables added to a clear broth or stock. All these methods are still used today.

Sauce Robert Bourgeoise

Menon, *La cuisiniere bourgeoise*, 1756, vol. 2, pages 257–258

"Put a little butter in a saucepan with a spoonful of flour [mixture]; brown the flour on a light fire, when it has a good colour, add three large very finely chopped onions and enough butter to cook them; moisten with bouillon, degrease the sauce and let it boil for half an hour. When you are ready to serve it, add salt, black pepper, a *filet* of vinegar, & mustard. You can use this sauce for fresh pork and turkey."

Sauceboat, England, Worcester, c. 1752–1754.
Soft-paste porcelain, enamels. Gardiner Museum, Toronto. Gift of Diana Gillespie

Onion Sauce Robert Bourgeoise

Inspired by Menon's recipe

INGREDIENTS
4 tbsp (60 g) butter
3 onions, finely chopped
3 tbsp (30 g) all-purpose flour
2 cups (500 ml) good beef broth or stock
1 tbsp (15 ml) red wine vinegar
1 tbsp (15 ml) Dijon mustard
Freshly ground pepper
Kosher salt, if needed

The All-Important *Bouillon*

Nothing was more fundamental to French cuisine than the preparation of *bouillon* (clear broth or stock), which required both time and care. Strapped for time, then as now, some chefs even purchased ready-made stock and reductions from other professional suppliers.[45] Marin's *bouillon* included bone-in shank of beef and a veal shank and a stewing hen, together with root vegetables. The keys to good *bouillon* were careful skimming, degreasing, and attention to temperature. Such stocks needed to simmer very gently for hours, but not boil. The result could be used to make more concentrated flavour enhancers, such as *jus* and *quintessences*.[46]

Pair of leaf-shaped sauceboats, England, Worcester, c. 1758–1760. Soft-paste porcelain, enamels. Gardiner Museum, Toronto. The Vernon W. Armstrong Collection

METHOD

· Melt 1 tbsp (15 g) of the butter in a frying pan. Cook the onions until they are very soft and beginning to brown. In a separate saucepan, melt the remaining butter and add the flour; stir the *roux* until it is golden-brown but not burnt. Add the stock to the *roux* gradually while stirring, so they are combined. Bring to a boil and add the onions. Simmer very gently for 15 minutes.

· Remove from heat and degrease the sauce with a sheet of paper towel (if fat is visible on the surface). Stir in the vinegar and the mustard. Adjust the seasoning by adding additional vinegar and freshly ground pepper to your taste. It may not be necessary to add salt.

Cerfeuillade, Sauce au poulet (Chervil Sauce for Chicken)

François Marin, *Les dons de Comus*, 1739, pages 168–169

"Simmer a piece of veal and ham with onion, carrot, parsnip and two cloves of garlic; moisten with good bouillon, oil and white wine. Let it all reduce to the quantity of a sauce: sieve and remove the oil; add the blanched, well chopped chervil with a small piece of butter about the size of a walnut, kneaded with flour, stir the sauce and serve."

Sauceboat, England, Bow, c. 1750. Soft-paste porcelain. Collection of Rosalie Wise Sharp

Chervil or Parsley Sauce for Chicken

Inspired by Marin's recipe

INGREDIENTS
1 medium onion, chopped
1 tbsp (15 ml) oil
4 oz (115 g) ground lean veal
4 oz (115 g) chopped ham (unsmoked or very lightly smoked)
1 large carrot, chopped
1 parsnip, chopped
2 cloves garlic, chopped
1/2 cup (125 ml) white wine
1 1/2 cups (355 ml) chicken stock
2 tbsp (30 g) butter
3 tbsp (30 g) flour
1/2 cup (12 g) chopped chervil or parsley
Kosher salt and freshly ground black pepper

METHOD
· Cook the onion in the oil for about 5 minutes in a frying pan until softened. Add the veal and ham and cook for a few minutes until the meat is no longer pink. Then add the vegetables. Continue cooking until the meat and vegetables start to brown, scraping the pan. Add the garlic and cook for a few more minutes.
· Add the wine and bring to a boil, then add the stock and season with salt and pepper; return to a boil. Remove any scum with a spoon if necessary. Simmer very gently for about 20 minutes until reduced by about a quarter.
· Sieve the sauce and discard the vegetables and meat. Either remove the fat from the surface of the stock with paper towel, or cool the stock and place in the fridge overnight; the following day, remove the solidified fat from the surface of the stock and discard.
· Heat the stock and gradually add the butter, kneaded with the flour, stirring all the time until the sauce thickens. Finish by adding the chopped parsley or chervil and season to taste with salt and pepper.

Desserts
AND Drinks

Fresh *Apricot* Compote

The large variety of fruit that was cultivated in Europe in the 1600s and 1700s enabled the wealthy to display the abundance of their gardens on their dessert tables. Pyramids of raw fruit were piled high on porcelain dishes, sometimes layered with plates of decreasing sizes to add stability, or the fruit was drizzled with caramel, or frozen in pyramidal forms (see illustration on page 114). Soft fruits, such as apricots, were also preserved with sugar. Compotes—fruit stewed gently with sugar—were particularly popular and were eaten by diners immediately after they were made. One anonymous cook described how compotes were "served hot on porcelains or bowls, which are today the most fashionable vessels for this."[49] Moulded fruit pastes and fruit marmalades were also popular desserts.

To Make a Compote of Apricots

Hannah Glasse, *The complete confectioner*, 1800
(facsimile of 2018), page 68

"Take any quantity of apricots, split them on one side to take out the stone, put them in a pan of water, and set them over the fire, boil them very gently for fear they should mash; when you see they are well softened, take them off and change them into cold water; take clarified sugar, put your apricots in, give them a little boiling, then take them off and set them in your dishes."

Nicolas de Bonnefons (dates unknown), translated by John Evelyn, Title page and frontispiece, *The French Gardiner, Instructing How to Cultivate all sorts of Fruit-Trees, ... Written Originally in French, and now Transplanted into English*, 3rd ed. London: S.S. for Benj. Tooke, 1672. Thomas Fisher Rare Book Library, University of Toronto

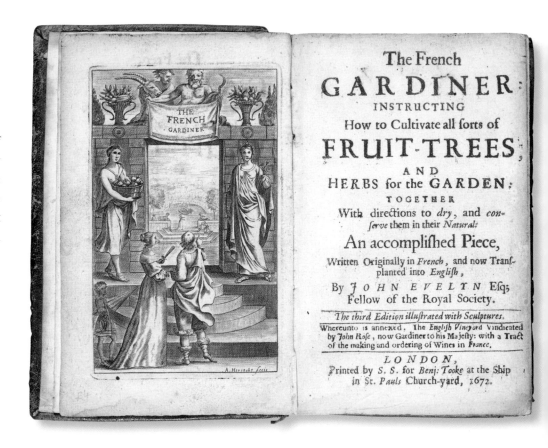

Fresh Apricot Compote

Inspired by Hannah Glasse's recipe
6 servings

INGREDIENTS
1 lb (450 g) pitted ripe apricots (avoid bruised or overripe fruit)
1 cup (250 ml) water
1 cup (200 g) sugar
Few drops of pure almond essence

METHOD
· Rinse the apricots. Remove their stones by making a slit in one side of each fruit and gently extracting. Try to preserve the whole form of the apricot as much as possible.
· Place the water and sugar in a saucepan over a low heat. Stir until the sugar is completely dissolved, then bring to a boil. Simmer for about 5 minutes without a lid.
· Add the apricots and simmer, without a lid, until the apricots are soft and still holding their form. Test with a fork. Remove the apricots from the syrup with a slotted spoon and place in a bowl. Boil the syrup for 4 or 5 minutes until it is reduced by almost one half. Add 3 or 4 drops of almond essence (no more) and stir. Let cool slightly, then pour over the apricots. Additional sauce can be served separately. Very good served with vanilla ice cream.

Gardener pruning a tree, Germany, Ludwigsburg, c. 1765. Model by Jean-Jacob Louis (1703–1772). Hard-paste porcelain, enamels, and gilding. Gardiner Museum, Toronto. The Hans Syz Collection

NOUVELLE
INSTRUCTION
POUR
LES CONFITURES;
Où l'on apprend à confire toute
forte de Fruits, tant au fec qu'au
liquide, & divers Ouvrages de
Sucre, & autres qui font du fait
des Confiſeurs & Officiers.

CHAPITRE PREMIER.
*Du choix du Sucre; la maniere de le
clarifier, & ſes différentes Cuiſſons.*

Choix du Sucre.

LE Sucre, qu'on veut employer, doit
être choiſi du plus beau & du plus
blanc, autant qu'on pourra; qu'il ſoit
A

Copy Cats

Most cookbook writers of the 1700s shamelessly copied recipes from their predecessors while always proclaiming that their own works were both superior and original. They also frequently disparaged the works they copied. Simple recipes, such as those for fruit compotes, hardly changed at all for over a hundred years; Hannah Glasse's recipe for apricot compote, which is quoted with this recipe, is identical to those used for many decades beforehand in both England and France.

François Massialot (1660–1733), Dessert table, *Le Confiturier Royal, ou, Nouvelle Instruction pour les Confitures, les liqueurs et les fruits,* 6th ed. Paris: s.n., 1791. Collection of Ivan Day

Lemon *Syllabub*

Syllabub was a favourite sweet treat popular in England from at least the 1600s. There are many different recipes: some called for sack (a sweet sherry), others for Rhenish (a fruity white wine), and some for a mixture of sack and Rhenish, claret, or even cider. One recipe suggests that instead of whisking the mixture into a froth, alcohol should be placed in a bowl and the cow milked directly over the top![47] Syllabubs were replaced by the more fashionable ice creams in the second half of the 1700s, but they were revived in England in the 1970s and are still popular today.

How to Make a Sullibub

Thomas Newington, *A Butler's Recipe Book*, 1719 (1935 edition), page 10

"Take a pint of Cream and a pint of Sack and Double Refine Lofe Sugar, take the whites of 2 Eggs, the juce of a lemon. Put all this in a bassoon, take a whisk and whip it. As the froth riseth take it off with a spoone. Put sugar on it."

Lemon tureen, Germany, Meissen, c. 1745–1750. Hard-paste porcelain, enamels. Gardiner Museum, Toronto. Gift of George and Helen Gardiner

Lemon Syllabub

Inspired by Thomas Newington's recipe
8 servings

INGREDIENTS
1 ripe lemon, juice and finely grated peel (washed first)
½ cup (100 g) sugar
1 cup (250 ml) fruity white wine, such as a Riesling or Alsatian
2 tbsp (30 ml) medium sherry, optional
2½ cups (590 ml) whipping or double cream
2 large egg whites

METHOD
· In a large bowl, or bowl of an electric mixer, add the lemon juice and peel, then add the sugar and stir together until the sugar is completely dissolved. Add the wine and the optional sherry. Whisk well while gradually adding in the cream; continue whisking (on medium-low if with an electric mixer) until the mixture begins to thicken or soft peaks just begin to form. Do not over whisk as the mixture will curdle very quickly. Taste and add more lemon, sugar, or wine if necessary. Whisk 2 egg whites to soft peaks and fold into the cream mixture. Spoon gently into wine glasses and refrigerate overnight.
· Overnight, the syllabub will divide into two sections: some liquor in the base with a creamy mousse–like top.

The *Terrible* Cost of Sugar

$\mathcal{T}$he dessert course was the climax of the meal in the 1700s: "During dessert the spirit revives, the wittiest words are spoken, the most agreeable topics debated ... which provide the greatest charm to life."[48] This vision of light-hearted pleasure completely obscures the terrible reality, as revealed in the painting by Philippe Mercier. It shows a group of carefree diners enjoying fruit and syllabub while a young black slave stands in service. The unquenchable appetite for sugar in Europe in the late 1600s and 1700s led to appalling human consequences. The British, French, Portuguese, Dutch, and Spanish forcibly enslaved and transported millions of Africans to the Caribbean Islands and Brazil to work on sugar plantations; innumerable others were forced to toil on plantations growing tobacco, cotton, indigo, and cacao in the Americas. Conditions of their transit and labour were brutal, degrading, and deadly. Abolitionists did not succeed in fully emancipating plantation slaves in the Caribbean until the 1840s; slavery was not abolished in Brazil until 1888.

Sweetmeat and syllabub glasses and stands, England, c. 1750–1775. Lead glass. Royal Ontario Museum, Toronto

OPPOSITE: Philippe Mercier (c. 1689–1760), *Sense of Taste,* 1744–1747. Oil on canvas. Yale Center for British Art, New Haven, Connecticut. The Paul Mellon Collection

Melon Fritters

Nicolas de Bonnefons considered melons "the most precious Fruit that your Kitchen Garden afford."[50] He went into great detail to show how to grow them in cold climates as far north as Paris. First, he advised gardeners to seek out the best seeds from Italy or southern France. Next, they should choose the best place in the garden for the *melonnière* and enclose the plant to secure it from winds. He advised the use of horse and donkey dung to warm and enrich the soil. The seeds were planted in tepid soil and "covered with pretty large Drinking Glasses," leaving a little space for air, to encourage the seedlings to sprout. Once transplanted into warm beds and nurtured under larger glass cloches, the melon plants would flourish until they were "weighty in the hand, firm to the touch … and of a Vermillion hue within."[51]

Melons

Nicolas de Bonnefons, *Les delices de la campagne, suite du jardinier françois…*, 1684, pages 102–103

"You can also cut them into slices and dip them into a batter (made with wheat flour, eggs, soft cheese and other ingredients …) then they are fried in fresh butter or lard: and when they are taken out of the pan, you powder them with salt or sugar, according to the taste of those to whom they are served: orange juice or lemon, verjus or a little vinegar is the best sauce for all fritters."

Sir Hans Sloane dish with melon and cherries, England, Chelsea, c. 1755. Soft-paste porcelain, enamels. Collection of Rosalie Wise Sharp

OPPOSITE: Nicolas de Bonnefons (dates unknown), translated by John Evelyn, Melon beds, *The French Gardiner, Instructing How to Cultivate all sorts of Fruit-Trees, … Written Originally in French, and now Transplanted into English,* 3rd ed. London: S.S. for Benj. Tooke, 1672. Thomas Fisher Rare Book Library, University of Toronto

Melon Fritters

Inspired by Nicolas de Bonnefons's recipe
6 to 8 servings

Marinating the melon in port enhances its flavour but is optional. When François Marin reprised this recipe, he suggested soaking the melon pieces in brandy and a little sugar.[52]

INGREDIENTS
1 small cantaloupe melon, not too ripe
1/2 cup (125 ml) port, optional
2 whole eggs
2/3 cup (160 ml) cup milk
1 tsp (5 g) salt
1 tbsp (15 g) sugar
1 cup (150 g) flour
2 egg whites
Soup bowl full of sugar
Lemon juice, optional

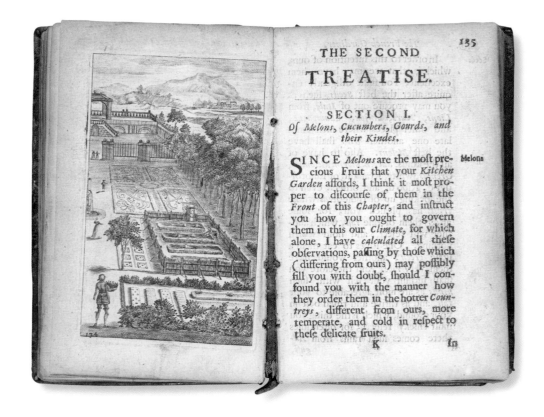

METHOD
· Cut the melon into bite-size cubes and marinate in the port. Place in the refrigerator at least 2 hours prior to making the fritters.
· Meanwhile, to make the batter: whisk the 2 whole eggs, milk, salt, and the sugar in a bowl. In another bowl, sift the flour and make a well in the middle. Pour in 2/3 of the egg and milk mixture and using a whisk gradually incorporate the flour, working from the middle to the outside edge. When almost all is incorporated, add the remaining egg and milk mixture and whisk vigorously to a smooth batter. Refrigerate for at least 2 hours.
· Meanwhile, remove the refrigerated melon from the port and place on a dish lined with plenty of paper towel; pat to dry.
· Beat the 2 egg whites until they hold their shape but are not stiff and fold gently into the batter. Put all the melon pieces in the batter. Heat the oil to 350 °F (175 °C), add the melon pieces, spoon by spoon, in batches, turning to ensure both sides are golden brown.
· Remove with a slotted spoon or tongs and immediately place in a bowl of sugar, turning the fritters over to coat all sides.
· Serve immediately. If desired, squeeze a little lemon juice over the top.

Artificial Melons

For those who lived too far north for melons to be grown successfully, Elizabeth Moxon told her readers how to make the most extraordinary artificial melon. It involved taking very lean sausage meat and colouring it green, "as near the colour of melon as possible," with spinach juice and herbs such as parsley that would enhance the green colour. Next, the coloured sausage meat was rolled out to about an inch thick and pressed into both sides of a large melon-shaped mould. She suggested packing the middle with stewed oysters. Once closed, the mould would be boiled in a cloth, "until you think it is enough." The "melon" was then released from the mould and served with a hot oyster sauce for either the first or the second course.[53] This remarkable recipe is typical of some dishes of the period that were not what they appeared to be!

Melon tureen, England, Chelsea, c. 1755. Soft-paste porcelain, enamels. Collection of Rosalie Wise Sharp

Brown Bread Ice Cream

Ices and ice creams were the most fashionable dessert of the second half of the 1700s. An extraordinary number of different flavours were made by cooks and confectioners, including sweet ices made of violets, ice creams flavoured with tea, and savoury ice cream made with Parmesan cheese. The recipe for Brown Bread Ice Cream first appeared in an English cookbook in 1770 and was quickly copied by other authors such as Mary Smith and in later editions of Hannah Glasse's cookbook.[54] It is still popular in England today.

Brown Bread Cream Ices

Hannah Glasse, *The complete confectioner*, 1800 (facsimile of 2018), pages 81–82

"Take any quantity of cream, prepare it as before, boiling it alone with yolks of eggs and the sugar, pass it through a sieve and put it in the sabotiere [*a sabotiere is a lidded metal container for freezing ice cream*]; when your cream begins to congeal, have crumbs of brown bread, which must be grated and sifted as fine as powder, put it in the sabotiere, and continue to work your cream for congealing. You may also make this sort of cream with plain cream alone, without yolks of eggs, or boiling, adding only a proper quantity of powdered loaf sugar, and set it to congeal, and when it begins to ice, then put [in] your sifted crumbs of brown bread; but take care to have it very finely sifted, for it renders it infinitely more agreeable to the mouth."

Brown Bread Ice Cream

Inspired by Hannah Glasse's recipe
8 to 10 servings

INGREDIENTS
4 egg yolks
½ cup (100 g) sugar
Pinch of kosher salt
2 cups (500 ml) heavy cream
1 cup (250 ml) whole milk
1½ tsp (7.5 ml) pure vanilla essence
1½ cups (75 g) brown bread crumbs
   (made with approximately 3 slices
   dry wholemeal bread, crusts removed)
½ cup (100 g) dark brown sugar
½ tsp (2.5 g) kosher salt

METHOD
· Whisk the egg yolks, sugar, and a pinch of salt together in a large bowl. Set aside.
· Warm the cream and milk in a saucepan until it is hot but not boiling. Very slowly and gradually pour the hot cream and milk into the egg mixture, whisking all the time and taking care not to let the mixture curdle.

Ice cream cooler with inner bowl and lid (*Seau à glace*), France, Sèvres, 1771. Soft-paste porcelain, enamels, and gilding. The Metropolitan Museum of Art, New York City. Gift of Mrs. William C. Breen, 1964

OPPOSITE: M. Emy (dates unknown), Frontispiece and title page showing putti making ice cream, *L'Art de bien faire les glaces d'Office ...*, 1st ed. Paris: Le Clerc, 1768. Collection of Ivan Day

· Wipe out the saucepan and pour in the egg and milk mixture; heat very gently, whisking constantly until the mixture begins to thicken (it should just coat the back of a spoon). Do not boil or overheat. Remove from stove and add the vanilla; whisk and immediately decant into a cold container. Place in the fridge to cool completely.

· Break the bread into small pieces. If necessary, dry out the bread in a low oven. Process in a food processor until bread crumbs are formed. Remove and mix together the bread crumbs, brown sugar, and salt.

· Heat the oven to 400 °F (200 °C). Cover a cookie sheet with aluminium foil, oil it lightly, and spread the crumb mixture over it evenly. Bake for about 10 minutes until caramelized and crispy; stir the crumbs if necessary. Watch so they do not burn. Remove the aluminium foil with the crumbs from the cookie sheet and allow to cool completely. Return the cold crumb mixture to the food processor and process for 1 or 2 seconds until fine crumbs are formed.

· Refrigerate the crumb mixture. Once the ice cream mixture is very cold, place it in the ice cream maker and turn on. Five to 10 minutes before it is set, add the bread crumbs, then continue until the ice cream is made.

· Decant the ice cream into a lidded, freezer-safe container. Freeze for at least 1 hour to help develop the flavour. Remove the container from the freezer and place in the fridge for half an hour before serving. Best eaten within 2 or 3 days.

L'Art de bien faire les Glaces

L'ART
DE BIEN FAIRE
LES GLACES D'OFFICE;
OU
LES VRAIS PRINCIPES
Pour congeler tous les Rafraichissemens.

*La maniere de préparer toutes sortes de
Compositions, la façon de les faire
prendre, d'en former des Fruits, Can-
nelons, & toutes sortes de Fromages.*

Le tout expliqué avec précision selon
l'usage actuel.

AVEC

UN TRAITÉ SUR LES MOUSSES.
*Ouvrage très-utile à ceux qui font des Glaces
ou Fromages glacés.*
Orné de Gravures en taille-douce.
Par M. EMY, *Officier.*

Prix, 2 liv. 10 sols *broché*; 3 liv. *relié.*

A PARIS,
Chez LE CLERC, Libraire, quai des
Augustins, à la Toison d'or.

M. DCC. LXVIII.
Avec Approbation & Privilege du Roi.

Ice and *Ice Cream*

Before the advent of refrigerators, labourers cut ice from rivers and lakes in winter and stored it in specially built ice houses. The wealthy constructed these buildings partially underground, in the coolest section of their gardens. Merchants also stored and sold ice in cities. Chipped ice was mixed with salt flakes and saltpetre to make ice cream freeze more quickly. Ice was also used in coolers to present ice cream at the table; ice was placed inside the cooler beneath a removable bowl, as well as in the rimmed lid to keep the ice cream frozen.[55]

The whole process of making ice cream can be seen in an illustration in M. Emy's publication on the art of making ices (see page 123); from ice houses to the pails for salt and ice, to the *sorbetières*—or as Hannah Glasse refers to it, a "sabotiere"—for freezing ice cream, and lastly the little cups for serving the frozen treat.

Four ice cream cups and a tray (*Tasses à glace, plateau Bouret*), France, Sèvres, 1770. Soft-paste porcelain, enamels, and gilding. Private collection, Toronto

Iced Oranges

The art of *trompe l'oeil*, or fooling the eye, was very popular in the mid-1700s, and many period recipes strive to make one type of food look like another. Ceramic manufacturers created a wide variety of vessels from tureens to teapots in the shape of animals, birds, fruits, and vegetables, all of which added to the fun. Ice cream was particularly suitable for this playful approach. A wide variety of pewter moulds for ice cream were available. Flavours and shapes could be mixed up to surprise the diner, as with this delicious recipe by Mary Smith for orange ice served in a pineapple mould.

Ice Cream another Way

Mary Smith, *The Complete House-keeper, and Professed Cook*, 1772, page 300

"Squeeze the juice of eight sweet oranges into a bowl, add to it half a pint of water and as much sugar as will sweeten it; strain it through a sieve, put it into an ice well, and freeze it 'till it is stiff; put it in a lead pine-apple mould, lap it well up in paper, put it into a pail of ice, and salt under and over it, and let it stand for three hours. When you want it, dip your pine-apple in cold water, turn it out on a plate, green the leaves of the pineapple with spinage juice, and garnish it with green leaves. You may put this cream into melon and pear moulds. If a melon, you must green it with spinage juice; if a pear mould, you must streak it with red."

Iced Oranges

Inspired by Mary Smith's recipe
Approximately 8 servings

INGREDIENTS
6 to 8 large oranges
1 cup (250 ml) water
1 cup (200 g) sugar
Juice of ½ lemon
Mint leaves for decoration

METHOD
- Wash the oranges carefully. Grate the rind of 2 of the oranges, then extract enough juice to make 2 cups (500 ml) of strained juice. Preserve 8 of the juiced orange halves in a plastic bag and freeze.
- Place the water, sugar, and finely grated orange rind in a saucepan over a low heat and stir until the sugar has dissolved completely. Boil for 2 minutes, then remove from the heat. Add in the strained orange and lemon juice.
- Refrigerate the mixture. When it is completely cold, place in an ice cream machine and freeze according to the manufacturer's directions.

The Pineapple House, Airth, Scotland. Built for John Murray, Fourth Earl of Dunmore, the last governor of the Colony of Virginia, as a hothouse for growing tropical fruit and as a summer house in 1761. The pineapple dome was an addition that probably dates to after 1776. National Trust for Scotland

· When almost set, decant into a freezer-safe container and leave to freeze for at least 1 hour. Check before serving: if the sorbet is frozen solid, place for half an hour in the refrigerator to soften a little. Just before serving, fill each of the 6 frozen orange halves with a generous scoop of sorbet, making a dome above the edge of the peel, so each resembles a half-peeled whole orange. Decorate with a small sprig of mint to imitate orange leaves and serve immediately.

Frozen Fruits

Naturalistic orange-shaped ices were a feature of an unbelievably extravagant *al fresco* dinner held in September 1754 at Schloss Hof, Austria, for the pleasure of Empress Maria Theresa and Emperor Francis I. For dessert, a garden was created on an artificial floating island in the lake: "The Prince had orange trees hung with ices in among the natural fruits, just as the rest of the island was bedecked in great abundance with a large quantity of sugary things, ices and all sorts of delicious refreshments."[56]

In Europe's northern climes, citrus and other tropical fruits were cultivated in hothouses. The rarest and most fashionable of these were pineapples, originally from South America. A few European gardeners succeeded in growing pineapples in the mid-1600s; the temperamental plants required constant heat for two years before fruiting. Pineapples became symbols of great wealth and could be rented for fashionable dinners in London if hosts did not have their own supply. They were so expensive that they were rarely eaten, which is why pineapple-shaped moulded desserts and ice creams were popular at the time.

Pineapple ice cream mould, probably English, early 1800s. Pewter. Collection of Ivan Day

Portugal Cakes

Kitchens in grand houses were divided into two sections in the 1700s: the main kitchen, where the preparation and cooking of savoury foods took place and where the principal fire for roasting food and the ovens were located, and the *office*, or confectionary kitchen, which had a cooler environment, perfect for making pastry, jellies, and ice creams. Because of this distinction, cookbooks for savoury and for sweet recipes were often published separately. However, in England, the second course included both savoury and sweet dishes, and some English cookbooks intended for modest households contained both savoury and sweet recipes together, such as those by Hannah Glasse and Elizabeth Raffald.

To Make Portugal Cakes

Hannah Glasse, *The Art of Cookery Made Plain and Easy*, 1769, 9th ed. (facsimile of 2018), page 274

"Mix into a pound of fine flour, a pound of loaf sugar beat and sifted, then rub it into a pound of pure sweet butter till it is thick like grated white bread, then put to it two spoonfuls of rose-water, two of sack, ten eggs, whip them very well with a whisk, then mix it into eight ounces of currants, mix'd all well together; butter the tin pans, fill them but half full, and bake them; if made without currants they will keep half a year; add a pound of almonds blanched, and beat with rose-water, as above, and leave out the flour. These are another sort and better."

Portugal Cakes

Inspired by Hannah Glasse's recipe
Approximately 20 small cakes, or 12 larger ones

INGREDIENTS
½ cup (75 g) dried currants, soaked in warm water to plump
2 generous cups (200 g) almond flour (all-purpose flour may be substituted)
1 cup (200 g) fine sugar
½ heaped tsp (3 g) kosher salt
1 cup (225 g) cold, unsalted butter, cut into small cubes
5 large eggs, separated
1 tbsp (15 ml) rose water, or orange-flower water (if neither are available, use 1 tbsp [15 ml] orange juice and the finely grated rind of ½ orange)
1 tbsp (15 ml) sweet sherry or port
Icing sugar for dusting

OPPOSITE: John Hugh Le Sage (c. 1694–c. 1749), Basket with the coat of arms of George II (r. 1727–1760), England, London, 1747. Silver. Royal Ontario Museum. Gift of Norman and Marion Robertson

METHOD

- Heat oven to 325 °F (165 °C). Line the small cake or muffin tins with paper cases and spray the interiors very lightly with oil.
- Soak the currants in warm water to plump them; set aside.
- Put the almond flour, sugar, and salt in the food processor with the butter and process for a few seconds until the butter forms small pea-size crumbs. Remove from the processor and place in a large bowl. Rub the mixture lightly with your fingers until it resembles large bread crumbs. (Alternately, you can do this entirely by hand.)
- Meanwhile, in the stand mixer, whisk the egg yolks until they are pale yellow in colour and have at least doubled in volume; this will take about 5 minutes. Then add in the rose water, or orange-flower water, and sherry (or sherry, orange juice, and orange rind) and continue to whisk for a few seconds until they are well incorporated.
- Combine the egg and flour mixtures with a spoon; the batter will be stiff. Rinse, drain, and dry the currants on a paper towel before stirring them into the batter.
- In a separate bowl, beat the egg whites until they are stiff. Take 2 large spoons of egg whites and mix them well into the batter; this will help to lighten the mixture. Then fold in the rest of the egg whites. Try to fold them so no egg whites remain visible while retaining as much volume as possible.
- Half fill the muffin cups or moulds. Bake muffin tins for about 30 to 35 minutes, smaller moulds for about 25 minutes. When done, the cakes will be golden brown on top and spring back when touched.
- Remove cakes from the tins and place on a rack to cool. When completely cold, dust with icing sugar before serving.
- Cakes can be kept for 2 days in a cookie tin.

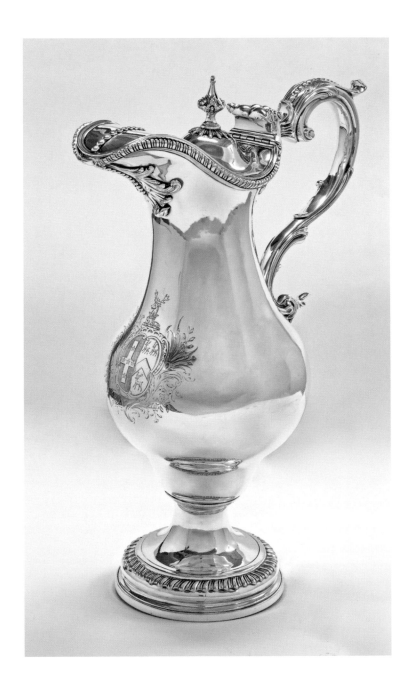

When to Eat *Little Cakes*

Small cakes such as these were a common element of the dessert course. It usually included a number of dishes, such as fresh fruit, compotes, small cakes, ice creams, jellies, and syllabubs, depending on the occasion and the household. For grand occasions, a centrepiece made of sugar could be created by the cook or rented from a confectioner and ornamented with porcelain sculptures and flowers, real or artificial.[57]

Small cakes were often served in a silver-handled basket. This basket was very convenient for teatime, which could be enjoyed *al fresco* or in a room inside. Cakes and toasting biscuits were also consumed by gentlemen while drinking sherry or port. It is possible that the name Portugal Cakes refers to the drink rather than the geographic origin of the cakes.[58]

Wine glass, France, 1700s. Blown glass. Collection of The Corning Museum of Glass, Corning, New York. Bequest of Jerome Strauss

OPPOSITE: William Grundy (active 1731–c. 1780). Wine jug, one of a pair, England, London, 1771. Silver. Anonymous gift, 1993. University of Toronto Art Collection. Courtesy of the Art Museum University of Toronto

Hot *Rum* Punch

Hot punch, made with brandy, rum, or arrack (a distilled alcohol produced in Asia), took the English by storm in the 1600s and 1700s. It was prepared in a large bowl and was shared. Punch was a social drink, particularly enjoyed by men. Delicious, convivial, and highly intoxicating, it led to raucous scenes in taverns, gentlemen's clubs, and private homes alike. This period was known for excessive drinking—gin was consumed in alarming quantities by the poor, while punch was quaffed by those who could afford it, along with fine claret, champagne, cognac, and port. John Nott even provides an extremely alcoholic (but no doubt delicious) recipe for Punch for Chambermaids in his cookbook, revealing that the beverage was also enjoyed by women.[59]

Punch Royal

John Nott, *The Cooks and Confectioners Dictionary*, 1724, unpaginated, recipe no. 266

"Take three Pints of best Brandy, as much Spring-water, a Pint or better of the best Lime-juice, a Pound of double refin'd Sugar. This Punch is better than weaker Punch, for it does not so easily affect the Head, by reason of the large Quantity of Lime-juice more than common, and it is more grateful and comfortable to the Stomach."

OPPOSITE: William Hogarth (1697–1764),
A Midnight Modern Conversation, c.1732.
Engraving on paper. Private collection

Hot Rum Punch

A slightly weaker version of John Nott's recipe

INGREDIENTS
8 or 9 ripe limes (to make one cup [250 ml] juice)
2 cups (400 g) sugar
3 cups (700 ml) Barbados rum
4 cups (950 ml) boiling water, or more depending on taste
Freshly grated nutmeg, to taste

METHOD
· Peel the limes, avoiding the white pith, and mix the peel with the sugar in a bowl, pressing down on the peels to release their oils. Let them sit for several hours or overnight to infuse.
· Place the sugar mixture in a small saucepan and remove the peel, pressing it against the side of the pan to extract as much oil and sugar as possible. Add 1 cup (250 ml) of the boiling water over a low heat; stir until the sugar is dissolved. Place this in a large heat-resistant punch bowl and add the lime juice and the rum, stirring well. Now add in 3 cups (700 ml) of the boiling water and mix well. Adjust for taste, adding more sugar or water if necessary. Lastly, add grated nutmeg to taste.
· Serve in small glass cups.

Celebratory *Punch Bowls*

Silver and porcelain punch bowls were frequently given as commemorative gifts. Many English and Chinese export porcelain punch bowls have inscriptions with patriotic verses, wishes for political victories, damnation to political foes, successes to enterprises and battles, or even commemorations of christenings and marriages. It is easy to imagine how these inscriptions may have encouraged toasts, further drinking, and general celebration.

Punch bowl, England, Staffordshire, 1783 or 1789. Pearlware, underglaze blue transfer print. Inscription: *Success to Wm Pitt / God Save the KING*. Gardiner Museum, Toronto. Gift of Dr. William Johnston in honour of the achievements of Meredith Chilton

Hot *Chocolate*

Along with tea and coffee, hot chocolate was a wildly fashionable and expensive drink in Europe during the 1600s and 1700s. Chocolate was usually prepared in special metal chocolate pots, some of which had holes in their lids so the *molinillo* (a special wooden whisk) could be inserted and rubbed between the hands; the beverage needed to be whisked briskly just before serving to amalgamate the natural fats in the chocolate. It was only in the early 1800s that the Dutch invented a process to remove some of the cacao butter from chocolate, which prevented the chocolate and its oils from separating. Chocolate was sometimes served in exquisite porcelain cups with galleried saucers, called *trembleuses*, to prevent the cups from tumbling over.

Comment préparer le Chocolat (How to Make Chocolate)

Anon., *L'École parfaite des Officiers de Bouche*, 1713, pages 203–204

"Chocolate is a mixture of drugs from which a beverage is made, & is also a remedy that came to us from Spain, who brought it from the Mexicans, among whom the word *chocolate* simply means *means* "confection."

"Chocolate is a composition of cacao, vanilla, cloves, cinnamon, mace & sugar. Once it is well prepared, a paste is made which you can use in the following manner. Put some water in a chocolate pot, let it boil; for four cups you take a *quarteron* of chocolate, or to proportion, also you can add sugar if you wish, all well grated, mix it well with the correct stick, then place it before the fire if you wish … taking care that it doesn't boil over.

"You must whisk it well with the stick to make a froth, & as it froths, so you pour your cups of chocolate, one after the other. If you want only one serving, you should add only a cup of water and one ounce of chocolate. If you wish, you can make chocolate with milk, add just the same amount as water, and boil first … You can lessen the amount of sugar if you don't like it to be so sweet."

Hot Chocolate in the Style of 1737

Inspired by the recipe in *L'École parfaite des Officiers de Bouche*
2 servings

INGREDIENTS
2 oz (60 g) 75 % good-quality dark chocolate
2 cups (500 ml) 3.25 % (full-fat) milk
1/2 vanilla pod
Sugar to taste
1/2 tsp (1 g) ground cinnamon
Tiny pinch ground cloves
Pinch ground mace, or freshly grated nutmeg
2 cinnamon sticks

METHOD
· Grate the chocolate or pulverize it in a food processor. Pour milk into a saucepan and scrape the inside seeds from the vanilla pod into the milk. Add the ground cinnamon, cloves, and mace or nutmeg; heat to almost boiling. Add the grated chocolate and whisk until dissolved. Pour into 2 cups and stir with the cinnamon sticks.

Johann Erhard Heuglin II (active 1717–1757), and others, Boxed set for breakfast, c. 1728–1729. Gilded silver, hard-paste porcelain, glass, and leather. The Sterling and Francine Clark Art Institute, Williamstown, Massachusetts. Acquired by the Clark Art Institute, 2012

Chocolate and *Breakfast Traditions*

As today, there were different breakfast traditions in Europe in the 1700s. The working classes ate gruel or bread and drank water, ale, or wine. The wealthy had more luxurious choices. In France, ladies could partake of a restorative meat *bouillon du matin* (morning broth) from a double-handled bowl known as an *écuelle*, while the bourgeois might enjoy hot chocolate or coffee.[60] In England, James Boswell (1740–1795) estimated that breakfast cost him £9 per year; he drank tea (which he kept locked up with his sugar) and ate bread, butter, and occasionally, marmalade.[61] In Italy, Pietro Longhi painted a Venetian lady and her morning visitors sipping chocolate and eating doughnuts.

Pietro Longhi (1701–1785), *The Morning Chocolate*, 1775–1780. Oil on canvas. Museo del Settecento Veneziano, Ca'Rezzonico, Venice

Chocolate beaker with *trembleuse* saucer, Beaker: Austria, Vienna, c. 1725; *trembleuse* saucer: possibly Austria or southern Germany, c. 1715–1735. Hard-paste porcelain, enamels, and gilding; tortoiseshell with gilt-metal mounts. Beaker: Gardiner Museum. Gift of George and Helen Gardiner; *Trembleuse* saucer: Gardiner Museum. Anonymous gift in memory of Henri Hickl-Szabo

NOTES ABOUT MEASUREMENTS

All cups are US cups (8 fluid ounces)

Equivalents of Pre-Revolutionary French measurements
found in recipes from 1650 to 1789:
Chopine: 2 US cups or ½ litre or 500 ml
Demi-septier: ½ US cup or ¼ pint or 125 ml
Quarteron: ¼ lb or 115 g

AUTHOR'S NOTE — DISCREPANCIES IN SPELLING

The historic English recipes in *The King's Peas* are reproduced with their original spelling and punctuation, which sometimes differs from the spelling of today; the French recipes have been transliterated by the author. At the time there was no standardization of spelling in either language, so cookbook authors often wrote words as they thought they were pronounced. For instance, "omelette" was spelled in different ways, including "aumelette" in French, and even "Amulet" and "Hamlet" in English.

Accents were also arbitrary. For ease of reading, accents have been added to French cookbook titles within the text. Titles however appear with their original spelling and accents in citations and in the bibliography.

OPPOSITE: Madame Tricot (Dominique Kaehler Schweizer, b. 1948), *A bundle of asparagus*, 2019. Hand-knitted wool. Collection of the artist

NOTES

1   Nicolas de Bonnefons, *Les delices de la campagne: Suitte du jardinier françois, ou est enseigné a preparer pour l'usage de la vie, tout ce qui croist sur la Terre, & dans les Eaux* (Paris: Pierre Des-Hayes, 1654), Epistre aux Dames.
2   Giacomo Casanova, *History of My Life*, vol. 4 (New York: Harcourt, Brace & World, 1966), 39.
3   Hannah Glasse, *The Art of Cookery, Made Plain and Easy; Which far exceeds any Thing of the Kind yet published.* 9th ed., 1769 (Pierceton, IN: Townsends, 2018), i and iv.
4   Glasse, *The Art of Cookery*, 15 and 18.
5   Charlotte-Elisabeth Orléans (duchesse d'), *Life and Letters of Charlotte Elizabeth: Princess Palatine and Mother of Philippe D'Orléans, Regent of France 1652–1722: Compiled, Translated, and Gathered from Various Published and Unpublished Sources* (London: Chapman and Hall, 1889), 266.
6   François Pierre de La Varenne, *Le cuisinier françois, enseignant la maniere de bien apprester et assaisonner toutes sortes de Viandes ... Legumes, ... par le sieur de La Varenne ...* (Paris: Pierre David, 1651), 284, http://gallica.bnf.fr/ark:/12148/bpt6k114423k.
7   Maguelonne Toussaint-Samat, *A History of Food* (Cambridge, MA: Blackwell Reference, 1993), 717–718.
8   Nicolas de Bonnefons, *The French Gardiner, Instructing How to Cultivate All Sorts of Fruit Trees, and Herbs for the Garden: ... Written Originally in French, and Now Transplanted into English* (London: Printed by S.S. for Benj. Tooke, 1672), 174.
9   Ibid., 180–181.
10 Susan Pinkard, *A Revolution in Taste: The Rise of French Cuisine, 1650–1800* (New York: Cambridge University Press, 2009), 195–199.
11 Louis-Auguste II de Bourbon, Prince de Dombes (attributed), "Epistle," *Le cuisinier gascon, Nouvelle edition, A laquelle on a joint la Lettre du Patissier Anglois* (Amsterdam: s.n., 1747). Louis Jules Barbon Mancini-Mazarini, duc de Nivernais (1716–1798) is also attributed as the author of *Le cuisinier gascon*, see The Sandy Michell Collection, Monash University Library, Melbourne.
12 Béatrix Saule, "Tables Royales à Versailles 1682–1789." In *Versailles et les tables royales en Europe: XVIIème–XIXème siècles: Musée national des châteaux de Versailles et de Trianon, 3 novembre 1993-27 février 1994*, ed. Musée national des châteaux de Versailles et de Trianon (Paris: Réunion des musées nationaux, 1993), 58.
13 Etienne Léon de La Mothe-Langon (baron) and Marie Jeanne Du Barry (comtesse), *Memoirs of Madame Du Barri [by E. L. de La Mothe-Langon] Tr. by the Translator of "Vidocq,"* vol. 31 (London: Whittaker, Treacher, and Arnot, 1830), 192.
14 Nicolas de Bonnefons, *Le jardinier françois, qui enseigne a cultiver les Arbres, & Herbes potageres; Auec la maniere de conseruer les Fruicts, & faire toutes sortes de Confitures, Conserues & Massepans* (Paris: Antoine de Sommauile, 1665), 125–127.
15 John Evelyn, *Acetaria: A Discourse of Sallets* (London: Printed for B. Tooke, 1699), 66.
16 Bonnefons, *Les delices de la campagne*, 1654, Epistre aux dames.
17 Ibid., 213.
18 Audiger, *La maison reglée et l'art de diriger la maison d'un grand Seigneur & autres, tant à la Ville qu'à la Campagne, & le devoir de tous les Officiers, & autres Domestiques en general* (Paris: Nicolas Le Gras, Augustin Besonge, Hilaire Foucault, 1692), 168–169.
19 Anne Willan, *Great Cooks and Their Recipes: From Taillevent to Escoffier* (New York: McGraw-Hill, 1977), 53.
20 Bonnefons, *The French Gardiner*, 157.
21 David Willey, "Police Files Expose Caravaggio Crimes," BBC News, Rome, February 18, 2011, https://www.bbc.com/news/world-europe-12497978.
22 Evelyn, *Acetaria*, 145.

23 Ibid., 173.

24 Ibid., 99–100.

25 W. H. Bidwell, ed., *The Eclectic Magazine of Foreign Literature, Science, and Art*, vol. 39 (Leavitt, Trow, & Company, 1856), 114–115.

26 Ibid.

27 Glasse, *The Art of Cookery*, 377.

28 Mary Smith, title page, in *The Complete House-keeper, and Professed Cook. Calculated For the greater Ease and Assistance of Ladies, House-keepers, Cooks, &c. &c. Containing upwards of Seven Hundred practical and approved Receipts…* (Newcastle: Printed by T. Slack, for the author, 1772).

29 Marie de Rabutin-Chantal Sévigné, Françoise Marguerite de Sévigné Grignan, and Sarah Josepha Buell Hale, *The Letters of Madame de Sévigné to Her Daughter and Friends*, rev. ed. (Boston: Roberts Brothers, 1878), 44–45.

30 Sara Paston-Williams and National Trust, *The Art of Dining: A History of Cooking & Eating* (London: National Trust 1999), 228.

31 James Boswell and Frederick A. Pottle, *Boswell's London Journal, 1762–1763: Now First Published from the Original Manuscript*, Yale Editions of the Private Papers of James Boswell (London: W. Heinemann, 1950), 51–52.

32 Ibid., 86.

33 Paston-Williams and National Trust, *The Art of Dining*, 204–205.

34 Daniel Roche, *France in the Enlightenment* (Cambridge, MA: Harvard University Press, 1998), 116–118.

35 Bourbon, Prince de Dombes, *Le cuisinier gascon*, 31, 36, 37, and 39; Silvano Serventi and Françoise Sabban, *Pasta: The Story of a Universal Food*, trans. Antony Shuggar (New York: Columbia University Press, 2002), 84.

36 Pinkard, *A Revolution in Taste*, 108–110.

37 Toussaint-Samat, *A History of Food*, 359–360.

38 Elizabeth Ann Williams, Meredith Chilton, and Los Angeles County Museum of Art, eds., *Daily Pleasures: French Ceramics from the MaryLou Boone Collection* (Los Angeles: Los Angeles County Museum of Art, 2012), 286.

39 Giacomo Casanova, *History of My Life*, vol. 5 (New York: Harcourt, Brace & World, 1966), 229–230.

40 Toussaint-Samat, *A History of Food*, 343.

41 Casanova, *History of My Life*, vol. 2 (New York: Harcourt, Brace & World, 1966), 103–104.

42 Menon (attributed), *The Art of Modern Cookery Displayed: Consisting of the most approved Methods of Cookery, Pastry, and Confectionary Of the Present Time: Translated from Les Soupers de la Cour, ou, La Cuisine Reformée, the last and most complete Practice of Cookery published in French*, trans. B. Clermont (London: Printed for the translator; sold by R. Davis, 1767), 30.

43 Glasse, *The Art of Cookery*, 91 and 191–194.

44 Pinkard, *A Revolution in Taste*, 111–119.

45 Ibid., 245.

46 Ibid., 244–245.

47 Hannah Glasse, *The complete confectioner; or, housekeeper's guide: To a simple and speedy Method of understanding the whole art of confectionary…* (London: Printed by J. W. Meyers, for West and Hughes, 1800), 184–185, http://nrs.harvard.edu/urn-3: HUL.FIG:008976826; and Ivan Day, "Further Musings on Syllabub, or Why Not 'Jumble It a Pritie While'?," in *Petits Propos Culinaires* 53 (1996), https://www.historicfood.com/Syllabubs%20Essay.pdf.

48 Meredith Chilton, "The Theatre of Dessert," in *Fired by Passion: Vienna Baroque Porcelain of Claudius Innocentius Du Paquier*, ed. Meredith Chilton and Claudia Lehner-Jobst (Stuttgart: Arnoldsche Art Publishers, 2009), 867.

49 Anon., *L'école parfaite des officiers de bouche: qui enseigne les devoirs du maître-d'hôtel, & du sommelier; la maniere de faire les confitures seches & liquides; les liquers, les eaux, les pommades & les parfums; la cuisine, à découper les viandes & à faire la patisserie*. 7th ed. (Paris: Pierre Ribou, 1708), 78.

50 Bonnefons, *Le jardinier françois*, 101.

51 Bonnefons, *The French Gardiner*, 134–152.

52 François Marin, *Suite des dons de Comus*, vol. 2 (Paris: Pissot etc., 1742), 455.

53 Elizabeth Moxon, *English Housewifery, exemplified in above Four Hundred and Fifty receipts, Giving Directions in most Parts of cookery…* 12th ed. (S.l.: s.n., 1778), 207–208.

54 Peter B. Brown et al., *Pleasures of the Table: Ritual and Display in the European Dining Room 1600–1900, An Exhibition at Fairfax House, York 1st September to 20th November 1997* (York: York Civic Trust, 1997), 87.

55 With thanks to Ivan Day for sharing information on ice cream and coolers.

56 Chilton and Lehner-Jobst, *Fired by Passion*, 860, with thanks to Claudia Lehner-Jobst.

57 Brown et al., *Pleasures of the Table*, 44–46.

58 Sarah B. Hood, "Portugal Cakes or Heart Cakes: A Recipe and Some History," *Eat Locally. Blog Globally* (blog), http://www.eatlocallyblogglobally.com/2013/03/portugal-cakes-or-heart-cakes-recipe.html.

59 John Nott, *The Cooks and Confectioners Dictionary: Or, The Accomplish'd Housewives Companion* (London: Printed by H. P. for C. Rivington, 1724), recipe no. 268.

60 Vincent La Chapelle, *Le cuisinier moderne, Qui aprend à donner toutes sortes de repas, En Gras & en Maigre, d'une manière plus délicate que ce qui en a été écrit jusqu'à present…* (La Haye: Antoine de Groot, aux dépens de l'auteur, 1736), 58.

61 Boswell and Pottle, *Boswell's London Journal, 1762–1763*, 230 and 335–336.

BIBLIOGRAPHY

Works cited:

Anon. *L'école parfaite des officiers de bouche: qui enseigne les devoirs du maître-d'hôtel, & du sommelier; la maniere de faire les confitures seches & liquides; les liquers, les eaux, les pommades & les parfums; la cuisine, à découper les viandes & à faire la patisserie.* 7th ed. Paris: Pierre Ribou, 1708.

———. *L'école parfaite des officiers de bouche: qui enseigne les devoirs du maître-d'hôtel, & du sommelier; la maniere de faire les confitures seches & liquides; les liquers, les eaux, les pommades & les parfums; la cuisine, à découper les viandes & à faire la patisserie.* 9th ed. Paris: Pierre Ribou, 1713.

———. *The Whole Duty of a Woman, or an Infallible Guide to the Fair Sex.* London: Printed for T. Read, 1737.

Audiger. *La maison reglée et l'art de diriger la maison d'un grand Seigneur & autres, tant à la Ville qu'à la Campagne, & le devoir de tous les Officiers, & autres Domestiques en general.* Paris: Nicolas Le Gras, Augustin Besonge, Hilaire Foucault, 1692.

Bidwell, W.H., ed. *The Eclectic Magazine of Foreign Literature, Science, and Art.* Vol. 39. Leavitt, Trow, & Company, 1856.

Bonnefons, Nicolas de. *Les delices de la campagne: Suitte du jardinier françois, ou est enseigné a preparer pour l'usage de la vie, tout ce qui croist sur la Terre, & dans les Eaux.* Paris: Pierre Des-Hayes, 1654.

———. *Les delices de la campagne, suite du jardinier françois: ou est enseigné a preparer pour l'usage de la vie, tout ce qui croist sur la terre & dans les eaux.* 6th ed. Augmentée par l'Autheur. Paris: Nicolas le Gras, 1684.

———. *Le jardinier françois, qui enseigne a cultiuer les Arbres, & Herbes Potageres; Auec la maniere de conseruer les Fruicts, & faire toutes sortes de Confitures, Conserues, & Massepans.* Paris: Antoine de Sommauile, 1665.

———. *Le jardinier françois, qui enseigne a cultiuer les Arbres, & Herbes Potageres; Auec la maniere de conseruer les Fruicts, & faire toutes sortes de Confitures, Conserues, & Massepans.* 8th ed. Paris: A. Cellier, 1666.

———. *The French Gardiner, Instructing How to Cultivate All Sorts of Fruit Trees, and Herbs for the Garden: ... Written Originally in French, and Now Transplanted into English.* 3rd ed. Translated by John Evelyn. London: Printed by S.S. for Benj. Tooke, 1672.

Boswell, James, and Frederick A. Pottle. *Boswell's London Journal, 1762–1763: Now First Published from the Original Manuscript.* Yale Editions of the Private Papers of James Boswell. London: W. Heinemann, 1950.

Bourbon, Louis-August II de, Prince de Dombes (attributed). *Le cuisinier gascon.* Nouvelle edition, *A laquelle on a joint la Lettre du Patissier Anglois.* Amsterdam: s.n., 1747.

Bradley, Martha. *The British Housewife: or, the Cook, Housekeeper's and Gardiner's Companion.* 2 vols. London: S. Crowder and H. Woodgate, 1760.

Brown, Peter B., Ivan Day, Fairfax House (York), and York Civic Trust. *Pleasures of the Table: Ritual and Display in the European Dining Room 1600–1900, An Exhibition at Fairfax House, York 1st September to 20th November 1997.* York: York Civic Trust, 1997.

Casanova, Giacomo. *History of My Life.* Vol. 2. New York: Harcourt, Brace & World, 1966.

———. *History of My Life.* Vol. 4. New York: Harcourt, Brace & World, 1966.

———. *History of My Life.* Vol. 5. New York: Harcourt, Brace & World, 1966.

Castelvetro, Giacomo. *The Fruit, Herbs and Vegetables of Italy: An Offering to Lucy, Countess of Bedford.* Translated by Gillian Riley. London: Viking, 1989.

Chilton, Meredith, and Claudia Lehner-Jobst, eds. *Fired by Passion: Vienna Baroque Porcelain of Claudius Innocentius Du Paquier.* Stuttgart: Arnoldsche Art Publishers, 2009.

Coe, Sophie D., and Michael D. Coe. *The True History of Chocolate.* Reprint. London: Thames and Hudson, 2006.

Day, Ivan. "Further Musings on Syllabub, or Why Not 'Jumble It a Pritie While'?" *Petits Propos Culinaires* 53 (1996). https://www.historicfood.com/Syllabubs%20Essay.pdf.

Emy, M. *L'Art de bien faire les glaces d'Office.* 1st ed. Paris: Le Clerc, 1768.

Evelyn, John. *Acetaria: A Discourse of Sallets.* London: Printed for B. Tooke, 1699.

Glasse, Hannah. *The Art of Cookery Made Plain and Easy; Which far exceeds any Thing of the Kind yet published.* New ed. London: W. Strahan et al, 1770.

———. *The Art of Cookery, Made Plain and Easy; Which Far Exceeds Any Thing of the Kind yet Published.* 9th ed., 1769. Pierceton, IN: Townsends, 2018.

———. *The complete confectioner; or, housekeeper's guide: To a simple and speedy Method of understanding the whole art of confectionary ...* London: Printed by J. W. Meyers, for West and Hughes, 1800. Middletown, DE: ULAN Press, 2018.

Hood, Sarah B. "Portugal Cakes or Heart Cakes: A Recipe and Some History." *Eat Locally. Blog Globally* (blog). Accessed February 27, 2019. http://www.eatlocallyblogglobally.com/2013/03/portugal-cakes-or-heart-cakes-recipe.html.

La Chapelle, Vincent. *Le cuisinier moderne, Qui aprend à donner toutes sortes de repas, En Gras & en Maigre, d'une manière plus délicate que ce qui en a été écrit jusqu'à present ...* La Haye: Antoine de Groot, aux dépens de l'auteur, 1736.

———. *The Modern Cook: Containing Instructions For Preparing and Ordering Publick Entertainments for the Tables of Princes, Ambassadors, Noblemen, and Magistrates.* 3rd ed. Vols. 1–3. London: Printed for Thomas Osborne, 1736.

La Varenne, François Pierre de. *Le cuisinier françois, enseignant la maniere de bien apprester et assaisonner toutes sortes de Viandes ... Legumes, ... par le sieur de La Varenne ...* Paris: P. David, 1651. http://gallica.bnf.fr/ark:/12148/bpt6k114423k.

———. *Le Vray Cuisinier François.* Brussels: G. de Backer, 1699.

———. *Le Vray Cuisinier François (Le Grand Ecuyer-Tranchant).* New ed. Brussels: G. de Backer, 1729.

Liger, Louis. *Le ménage des champs et de la ville, ou, nouveau cuisinier françois: Accommodé au goût du temps: Contenant tout ce qu'un parfait Chef de Cuisine doit savoir pour servir toutes sortes de Tables, depuis celles des plus grands Seigneurs jusqu'à celles des bons Bourgeois; avec une Instruction pour faire toutes sortes de Pâtisseries, Confitures seches & liquides, & toutes les différentes liqueurs qui sont aujourd'hui en usage.* Nouvelle édition. Paris: Christ. David, libraire-imprimeur, 1764.

Marin, François. *Les dons de Comus, ou, Les délices de la table.* Paris: Prault fils, 1739.

———. *Suite des dons de Comus, ou l'art de la cuisine, reduit en pratique.* Vol. 1 & 2. Paris: La veuve Pissot, Didot, Brunet fils, 1742.

Massiolot, François. *Le confiturier royal, ou, Nouvelle instruction pour les confitures, les liqueurs et les fruits: où l'on apprend à confire toutes sortes de fruits, tant secs que liquids; la façon de faire différens ratafias, & divers ouvrages de sucre que font du fait des officiers & confiseurs; avec la manière de bien ordonner un fruit.* 6th ed. Paris: s.n., 1791.

Menon (attributed). *The Art of Modern Cookery Displayed: Consisting of the most approved Methods of Cookery, Pastry, and Confectionary Of the Present Time. Translated from Les Soupers de la Cour, ou, La Cuisine Reformée, the last and most complete Practice of Cookery published in French.* Translated by B. Clermont. London: Printed for the translator; sold by R. Davis, 1767.

Menon. *La cuisiniere bourgeoise: suivie de l'office, a l'usage de tous ceux qui se mêlent de dépenses de Maisons.* 2 vols. Paris: Guillyn, 1756.

———. *La cuisiniere bourgeoise,* New ed. Amsterdam: aux dépans de la Compagnie, 1756.

Mothe-Langon (baron), Etienne Léon de La, and Marie Jeanne Du Barry (comtesse). *Memoirs of Madame Du Barri [by E. L. de La Mothe-Langon] Tr. by the Translator of "Vidocq".* Vol. 31. London: Whittaker, Treacher, and Arnot, 1830.

Moxon, Elizabeth. *English Housewifery, exemplified in above Four Hundred and Fifty receipts, Giving Directions in most Parts of cookery ...* 12th ed. S.l.: s.n., 1778.

Newington, Thomas. *A Butler's Recipe Book, 1719.* Cambridge: Cambridge University Press, 1935.

Nott, John. *The Cooks and Confectioners Dictionary: Or, The Accomplish'd Housewives Companion.* London: Printed by H. P. for C. Rivington, 1724.

Orléans (duchesse d'), Charlotte-Elisabeth. *Life and Letters of Charlotte Elizabeth: Princess Palatine and Mother of Philippe D'Orléans, Regent of France 1652–1722: Compiled, Translated, and Gathered from Various Published and Unpublished Sources.* London: Chapman and Hall, 1889.

Paston-Williams, Sara, and National Trust. *The Art of Dining: A History of Cooking & Eating.* London: National Trust, 1999.

Pennington, Mrs. *The Royal Cook; or, the Modern Etiquette of the Table, displayed with Accuracy, Elegance, and Taste.* London: Richard Snagg, 1774.

Pinkard, Susan. *A Revolution in Taste: The Rise of French Cuisine, 1650–1800.* Cambridge: Cambridge University Press, 2009.

Raffald, Elizabeth. *The Experienced English House-Keeper: For the Use and Ease of Ladies, House-Keepers, Cooks, &c. Wrote Purely from Practice, And dedicated to the Hon. Lady Elizabeth Warburton, Whom the Author lately served as House-Keeper.* Manchester: Printed by J. Harrop, for the author, and sold by Messrs. Fletcher and Anderson, in St. Paul's Church-Yard, London, and by Eliz. Raffald, Confectioner, near the Exchange, Manchester, 1769.

———. *The Experienced English Housekeeper, For the use and ease of Ladies, Housekeepers, Cooks, &c.* 9th ed. London: Printed for R. Baldwin, 1784.

Roche, Daniel. *France in the Enlightenment.* Vol. 130 of *Harvard Historical Studies.* Cambridge, MA: Harvard University Press, 1998.

Saule, Béatrix. "Tables Royales à Versailles 1682–1789." In *Versailles et les tables royales en Europe. XVIIème–XIXème siècles. Musée national des châteaux de Versailles et de Trianon, 3 novembre 1993-27 février 1994.* Edited by Musée national des châteaux de Versailles et de Trianon. Paris: Réunion des musées nationaux, 1993.

Serventi, Silvano, and Françoise Sabban. *Pasta: The Story of a Universal Food.* New York: Columbia University Press, 2002.

Sévigné, Marie de Rabutin-Chantal, Françoise Marguerite de Sévigné Grignan, and Sarah Josepha Buell Hale. *The Letters of Madame de Sévigné to Her Daughter and Friends.* Rev. ed. Boston: Roberts Brothers, 1878.

Smith, Mary. *The Complete House-keeper, and Professed Cook. Calculated For the greater Ease and Assistance of Ladies, House-keepers, Cooks, &c. &c. Containing upwards of Seven Hundred practical and approved Receipts ...* Newcastle: Printed by T. Slack, for the author, 1772.

Toussaint-Samat, Maguelonne. *A History of Food.* Cambridge, MA: Blackwell Reference, 1993.

Willan, Anne. *Great Cooks and Their Recipes: From Taillevent to Escoffier.* New York: McGraw-Hill, 1977. http://nrs.harvard.edu/urn-3:RAD.SCHL:33073526.

Willey, David. "Police Files Expose Caravaggio Crimes." February 18, 2011. BBC News, Rome. https://www.bbc.com/news/world-europe-12497978.

Williams, Elizabeth Ann, Meredith Chilton, and Los Angeles County Museum of Art, eds. *Daily Pleasures: French Ceramics from the MaryLou Boone Collection.* Los Angeles: Los Angeles County Museum of Art, 2012.

Works Consulted:

Bursche, Stefan. *Tafelzier des Barock.* Munich: Editions Schneider GmbH, 1974.

Camporesi, Piero. *Exotic Brew: The Art of Living in the Age of Enlightenment.* Cambridge: Polity Press, 1998.

Cassidy-Geiger, Maureen, ed. *Fragile Diplomacy: Meissen Porcelain for European Courts ca. 1710–63.* New Haven: Published for The Bard Graduate Center for Studies in the Decorative Arts, Design, and Culture, New York, by Yale University Press, 2007.

Ilchman, Frederick, Thomas S. Michie, C. D. Dickerson, Esther Bell, Museum of Fine Arts, Boston, Kimbell Art Museum, Fine Arts Museums of San Francisco, and Legion of Honor (San Francisco, Calif.), eds. *Casanova: The Seduction of Europe.* 1st ed. Boston, MA: MFA Publications, Museum of Fine Arts, Boston, 2017.

Lehmann, Gilly. *The British Housewife: Cookery Books, Cooking and Society in Eighteenth-Century England.* Totnes, Devon: Prospect Books, 2003.

L. S. R. *L'art de bien traiter, divisé en trois parties: Ouvrage nouveau, curieux et fort galant, utile a toutes personnes, et conditions: Exactement recherché, & mis en lumiere.* Lyons: Claude Bachelu, 1674.

Miles, Elizabeth B. *English Silver: The Elizabeth B. Miles Collection.* Hartford: Wadsworth Atheneum, 1976.

Peterson, T. Sarah. *Acquired Taste: The French Origins of Modern Cooking.* Ithaca: Cornell University Press, 1994.

Roth, Linda H., and Clare Le Corbeiller. *French Eighteenth-Century Porcelain at the Wadsworth Atheneum: The J. Pierpont Morgan Collection.* Hartford: Trustees of the Wadsworth Atheneum, 2000.

Sharp, Rosalie Wise. *China to Light Up a House.* Vol. 1. Toronto: ECW Press, 2015.

Vence, Céline, Robert J. Courtine, Philip Hyman, and Mary Hyman. *The Grand Masters of French Cuisine: Five Centuries of Great Cooking: Recipes.* New York: Putnam, 1978.

Wees, Beth Carver. *English, Irish, & Scottish Silver at the Sterling and Francine Clark Art Institute.* 1st ed. New York: Hudson Hills Press, 1997.

Wheaton, Barbara Ketcham. *Savoring the Past: The French Kitchen and Table from 1300 to 1789.* Philadelphia: University of Pennsylvania Press, 1983.

AUTHOR'S ACKNOWLEDGEMENTS

First, kudos must go to the great cooks of the 1600s and 1700s whose genius continues to inspire cuisine today. Particular thanks go to Ivan Day and to the many scholars whose publications were fundamental to *The King's Peas: Delectable Recipes and Their Stories from the Age of Enlightenment* and the exhibition it accompanies, *Savour: Food Culture in the Age of Enlightenment*. Among them are Peter Brown, Stephan Bursche, Sophie D. and Michael D. Coe, Gilly Lehmann, Sarah Paston-Williams, T. Sarah Peterson, Susan Pinkard, David Roche, Béatrix Saule, Maguelone Toussant-Samat, Ann Willan, and Barbara Ketcham Wheaton.

For their enthusiasm and support, heartfelt appreciation is due to our Co-Presenting Sponsors: Mary Janigan and Tom Kierans; Noreen Taylor and David Staines.

And sincere thanks go to all those who contributed to the publication: Markus Bestig, Executive Chef, The York Club, Toronto, who contributed four recipes, and Karine Tsoumis, curator at the Gardiner Museum and author of the Preface. My gratitude also goes to the recipe testers: Charles Almond, Francine Boivin, Thomas Chilton, Ross Flintoft, Jenny Paterson Jonas, Andrew Sharp, and Kathy Whitewick.

Thanks to the contemporary artists whose work is represented here or in the exhibition: Chris Antemann, Ivan Day, the late Joe Fafard, Gerard Gauci, Loraine Krell, Kate Malone, Janet Panabaker, and Madame Tricot (Dominique Kaehler Schweizer).

Grateful thanks also go to the many institutions, colleagues, friends, and private collectors who have made the cookbook and the exhibition possible: Thomas Aitken and Kate Hyde; Ellenor Alcorn, Art Institute of Chicago; Marylène Altieri, Diana Carey, and Ellen M. Shea, Arthur & Elizabeth Schlesinger Library on the History of Women in America, Harvard University; Dita Amory, Manus Gallagher, Iris Moon, Denny Stone, and Stephan Wolohojian, The Metropolitan Museum of Art; Michele Beiny; Carol Burnham Cook, Anne Dondertman, and Susan Johnston, Gardiner Museum Library; Mary Busick, Thomas L. Loughman, Allen Phillips, Linda Roth, and Vanessa Sigalas, Wadsworth Atheneum Museum of Art; Pearce Carefoote and Linda Joy, Thomas Fisher Rare Book Library, University of Toronto; Guy Coté; Andrew Kear and Nicole Fletcher, Winnipeg Art Gallery; Cyril Duport, The York Club, Toronto; Christopher Etheridge, National Gallery of Canada; Leslie Ferrin, Ferrin Contemporary; Anne Garner and Arlene Shaner, New York Academy of Medicine; Alexis Goodin, Chris Hightower, and Kathleen Morris, Sterling and Francine Clark Art Institute; Wulf Higgins, Canadian Opera Company; Dr. William Johnston; Peter Kaellgren and Robert Little, Royal Ontario Museum; Dan Liebman; Katharine Lochnan; Lars Kokkonen and Matthew Hargraves, Yale Center for the Study of British Art; Amanda Lang, Historic Deerfield; Edward Maeder; Christopher Maxwell, Corning Museum of Glass; Natasha Minaeva; Thomas Michie, Museum of Fine Arts, Boston; Peter Perina, Pavel Slavko, Český Krumlov Castle; Heather Darling Pigat, University of Toronto Art Centre; Marshall Pynkoski and Jeannette Lajeunesse Zingg, Opera Atelier; Cynthia Roman, Lewis Walpole Library; Adrian Sassoon and Min Weguelin; Rosalie Wise Sharp; Alan Shimmerman; Ivars Taurins; and Marlene Wilson; special thanks also to the private collectors whose generous participation has been so vital for this project.

Personal thanks are due to the outstanding exhibition team for *Savour: Food Culture in the Age of Enlightenment*: visionary exhibition designer Gerard Gauci and, from the Gardiner Museum, major exhibition manager Natalie Hume, along with curatorial installation manager Micah Donovan, art director Tara Fillion, chief curator Sequoia Miller, and curator Karine Tsoumis, together with Meria Faidi and Barbara Glaser. Other key Gardiner colleagues include Siobhan Boyd, Lauren Gould, Mary Kim, Adeline La, Christina MacDonald, Rea McNamara, Alice Stratford-Kurus, Richard Tang, Sophie Vayro, Rachel Weiner, and Celia Zhang. Further thanks to Thomas L. Loughman and Linda Roth, who have made it possible for the exhibition to travel to the Wadsworth Atheneum Museum of Art in 2020.

Sincere appreciation goes to the superb work of the publication teams for *The King's Peas* at the Gardiner Museum and Arnoldsche Art Publishers, along with independent specialists: publication managers Greta Garle, Arnoldsche, and Karine Tsoumis, Gardiner Museum; photo and permission manager Natalie Hume, Gardiner Museum; editors Wendy Brouwer, Thomas Chilton, Paula Sarson, Rosemary Shipton, and Karine Tsoumis; publication designer Karina Moschke; and publisher Dirk Allgaier, Arnoldsche. It has been an honour and a pleasure to work together with you all.

I cannot end without emphasizing my particular gratitude to Karine Tsoumis for her guidance and contributions to both the exhibition and the publication, and to my son, Thomas Chilton. Finally, many thanks to Executive Director and CEO Kelvin Browne and to the Board of the Gardiner Museum, whose ongoing support has been essential.

Meredith Chilton, C.M.
Curator Emerita, Gardiner Museum

This book is published in conjunction with the exhibition *Savour: Food Culture in the Age of Enlightenment*, organized by the Gardiner Museum, Toronto, and presented at the Gardiner Museum, Toronto (October 17, 2019–January 19, 2020) and the Wadsworth Atheneum Museum of Art, Hartford (February 29, 2020–May 24, 2020).

PUBLISHED FOR
The Gardiner Museum, Toronto, Canada

AUTHOR
Meredith Chilton, Lac-Brome, Canada

CONTRIBUTOR
Markus Bestig, Executive Chef, The York Club, Toronto, Canada

CONCEPT
Meredith Chilton, Lac-Brome, Canada

PROJECT MANAGEMENT
Karine Tsoumis, Toronto, Canada

PHOTO AND PERMISSION MANAGEMENT
Natalie Hume, Toronto, Canada

EDITING
Wendy Brouwer, Stuttgart, Germany
Thomas Chilton, Lac-Brome, Canada
Paula Sarson, Middle Sackville, Canada
Rosemary Shipton, Toronto, Canada
Karine Tsoumis, Toronto, Canada

ARNOLDSCHE PROJECT MANAGEMENT
Greta Garle, Stuttgart, Germany

GRAPHIC DESIGNER
Karina Moschke, Stuttgart, Germany

OFFSET REPRODUCTIONS
Schwabenrepro, Stuttgart, Germany

PRINTED BY
DZS Grafik, Ljubljana, Slovenia

BIBLIOGRAPHIC INFORMATION published by the Deutsche Nationalbibliothek
The Deutsche Nationalbibliothek lists this publication in the Deutsche Nationalbibliografie; detailed bibliographic data are available on the Internet at www.dnb.de.

ISBN 978-3-89790-560-3
www.arnoldsche.com

Made in Europe, 2019

PHOTO CREDITS
The Metropolitan Museum of Art, New York City: pp. 6, 10, 16, 22, 29, 35, 47, 105, 122; Michele Beiny/Richard Goodbody: pp. 9, 32, 64, 79, 98, 103; Richard Goodbody: p. 12; Gardiner Museum/Toni Hafkenscheid: pp. 5, 13, 15, 21, 23–24, 33, 40, 42–43, 48, 54, 60, 66, 68, 71–73, 80, 83, 85–86, 92 right, 95, 100, 108–111, 113–115, 118, 120–121, 123–125, 127, 133–134, 137 bottom; Gardiner Museum/Micah Donovan: Cover of cookbook, p. 19; University of Toronto Art Centre/Toni Hafkenscheid: p. 130; Thomas Fisher Rare Book Library, University of Toronto: pp. 14, 33, 59, 77, 88, 104, 112, 119; Ernest Mayer, courtesy of the Winnipeg Art Gallery: p. 17; Yale Center for British Art, New Haven, Connecticut: pp. 18, 58, 117; Bridgeman Images: pp. 20, 25, 26, 37, 49, 62, 96–97, 137 top; © S. Bianchetti/Bridgeman Images: p. 27; VectorStock: p. 28; The Stapleton Collection/Bridgeman Images: p. 56; Cameraphoto Arte Venezia/Bridgeman Images: p. 65 top; © RMN-Grand Palais/Art Resource, NY: p. 82; Uppsala Auktions Kammare, Sweden: p. 31; Madame Tricot/Daniel Ammann: pp. 36, 51, 61, 75, 139; Royal Ontario Museum © ROM: pp. 39, 67, 107, 116, 129; Michele Beiny/Laurence Rundell: p. 44; Allen Phillips: pp. 45, 52; Allen Phillips/Wadsworth Atheneum Museum of Art: pp. 53, 57, 69, 87, 101; © 2019 Museum of Fine Arts, Boston: pp. 55, 91; © The Royal Society, London: p. 65 bottom; Courtesy of the Clark Institute, Williamstown, Massachusetts: pp. 76, 94, 136; © 2019 Museum Associates/LACMA. Licensed by Art Resource, NY: p. 84; Schlesinger Library, Radcliffe Institute, Harvard University, Cambridge, Massachusetts: p. 92 left; Giannandrea: p. 126; Corning Museum of Glass, Corning, New York: p. 131

COVER ILLUSTRATIONS
FRONT: Cabbage tureen, France, Strasbourg, Paul Hannong, c. 1744–1754. Model attributed to Wilhelm Lanz (active 1748–1761). Tin-glazed earthenware (faïence). Private collection
Pea pod, England, Derby, c. 1770. Soft-paste porcelain, enamels. Gardiner Museum, Toronto. Gift of Mr. and Mrs. J.H. Moore
BACK: Small artichoke tureens, France, poss. Strasbourg, c. 1750. Tin-glazed earthenware (faïence). Private collection

FRONTISPIECE
Gerard Gauci (b. 1959), *Kitchen Garden Perspective*, 2019. Acrylic on board. Collection of the artist

CO-PRESENTING SPONSORS
Tom Kierans & Mary Janigan
Noreen Taylor & David Staines

Canada Council Conseil des Arts
for the Arts du Canada

ONTARIO ARTS COUNCIL
CONSEIL DES ARTS DE L'ONTARIO

 TORONTO   Ontario

 Gardiner Museum  WADSWORTH ATHENEUM MUSEUM OF ART